S'awright?

dummy days

America's Favorite Ventriloquists from Radio and Early TV

Scotty watty doo doo daa!

*When I get smitten,
I stay smut.*

*Alphabet soup is
very educational.*

*Dee-fee-cult for you.
Easy for me.*

Timmm-BER!

FLIP CLIP

dummy days

America's Favorite Ventriloquists from Radio and Early TV

kelly asbury

foreword by leonard maltin

afterword by jeff dunham

design by amy inouye

ANGEL CITY PRESS

SANTA MONICA

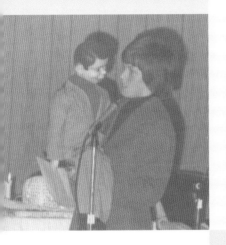

Above:
Al Getler with
Danny O'Day, 1973.

Left:
Linda Holliday with
Jerry Mahoney, 1958.

Below:
Michael Valentine with
Charlie McCarthy, 1971.

These kids pictured
here all grew up to
be professional
ventriloquists.

ANGEL CITY PRESS
2118 Wilshire Boulevard #880
Santa Monica, California 90403
310.395.9982
www.angelcitypress.com

Dummy Days:
America's Favorite Ventriloquists from Radio and Early TV
by Kelly Asbury
Copyright © 2003 by Kelly Asbury

Foreword © 2003 by Leonard Maltin

Afterword © 2003 by Jeff Dunham

Design by Amy Inouye

First edition
10 9 8 7 6 5 4 3 2 1

ISBN 1-883318-28-9

LIBRARY OF CONGRESS CATALOGING-IN-PUBLICATION DATA

Asbury, Kelly.
Dummy days : America's favorite ventriloquists from radio and early TV
/ by Kelly Asbury.
p. cm.

ISBN 1-883318-28-9 (hardcover : alk. paper)

1. Ventriloquists -- United States -- Biography.
I. Title.

PN2285.A83 2003
793.8'9'092273--dc21   2003005560

Printed in China

FLIP CLIP

With great admiration and gratitude to Jimmy Nelson,
"Gentleman Jim" himself, who created
my boyhood pals, Danny O'Day and Farfel,

and

In loving memory of my aunt, Melda Moy,
who sat me down in 1966 with a pen and the Sears catalog,
letting me circle the one toy I wanted most for Christmas.

—K.A.

FLIP = CLIP

contents

foreword

Leonard Maltin with Jimmy Nelson and Farfel at the 1998 Las Vegas Ventriloquist Festival, where Maltin presented Nelson with a special Life Achievement Award.

Comedy writer Larry Gelbart once observed, "When vaudeville died, television was the box they buried it in." I, for one, feel lucky that I grew up in that era of extended vaudeville that was early television. I loved watching great entertainers on TV when such opportunities were everyday occurrences on local kiddie shows and prime-time variety hours, including Ed Sullivan's fabled Sunday night program. Singers, comedians, tap dancers, jugglers and, of course, ventriloquists were all part of the regular bill of fare, and the best ones became part of our national consciousness.

In that simpler time, before the Internet and the two-hundred-channel TV universe, there wasn't a man, woman or child who didn't know Señor Wences. Every red-blooded boy or girl I knew watched Saturday morning TV and smiled as Farfel sang the praises of "N-E-S-T-L-E-S Chaw-claaaat." Paul Winchell and Shari Lewis seemed like friends of the family.

As time went on, television changed along with our society. *The Ed Sullivan Show* went away, as did the other variety programs; acts that had been a staple of vaudeville-bred entertainment faded from the scene. Kiddie-show hosts gave way to cartoons and reruns of old TV series. TV became more homogenized and less personal.

I am unabashedly, unapologetically nostalgic about those days—and I'm not alone. Whenever there's a gathering of aging Baby Boomers and the subject of 1950s and 1960s television comes up, you can sense the group going into a kind of trance, transporting themselves back in time. The memories are indelible.

I also believe that this form of entertainment is just as effective today as it ever was. When Señor Wences came to Los Angeles to appear in Milt Larsen's show *It's Magic* in 1983, I sat in a theater packed with children and their parents and listened to them scream with delight as he went through his paces. When my daughter Jessie was six, I took her along when I interviewed Shari Lewis about her remarkable television comeback—and saw her eyes light up when Shari presented her with a Lamb Chop of her very own. (Realizing that I was probably six when I first discovered Shari, I teased the wonderful performer about having a Dorian Gray-like 8-by-10 tucked away somewhere, grown old while she remained ageless. She told me that people often asked if she was "the original Shari Lewis.")

FLIP CLIP

Paul Winchell and Jimmy Nelson were a vivid part of my childhood. My friends and I imitated Farfel, and I took great delight in performing with my own Jerry Mahoney dummy. I even owned a record album—remember those?—that Paul and Jerry made called *Chips of Wisdom.*

Edgar Bergen, who inspired an entire generation of ventriloquists, was past his prime when I was young, and I never really cottoned to him—especially since it always seemed as though his lips were moving. Not until I grew older did I come to appreciate Bergen's enormous talent as a comedy writer and performer. I will never forget one of his last television appearances, on *The Tonight Show Starring Johnny Carson*; he was sharp, funny, and full of surprises. Carson was delighted, and so was the audience.

I have been luckier than many of my contemporaries because I've gotten to meet many of these ventriloquists; one couldn't ask for a nicer, more interesting group of people. My hat goes off to Kelly Asbury for paying the vents proper tribute and setting their stories down in print for all time. They are to be celebrated and cherished.

Since everything in life is cyclical, we may yet live to see ventriloquists return to mainstream entertainment. (Even the accordion seems to be making something of a comeback!) If that happy day should arrive, the entertainers who achieve success will surely know that they are standing on the shoulders of those who went before them: gifted people who brought untold happiness to generations of fans.

— LEONARD MALTIN

Leonard Maltin with Señor Wences
and his famous head-in-the-box,
Pedro, in Los Angeles, 1983.

9

introduction

I n the mid 1950s, long before Barbie or Ken dolls, *Star Wars* figures or computer games, one of the Big Toys for a kid was a "speaking doll" named Jerry Mahoney. Wearing a pint-sized plaid sports jacket and bow tie, the shiny, round-cheeked puppet had bright red hair and big brown eyes. More importantly, he also had a broadly smiling slotted mouth that opened and closed with the pull of a string on his back. Sewn on the lapel of his jacket was a tiny cloth label that read "Paul Winchell's Jerry Mahoney," a reminder of the famous ventriloquist who brought his wooden sidekick to life.

That Jerry Mahoney doll was at the top of many a child's Christmas list back then and was a best-selling toy of the era. Jerry joined the ranks of other dummy dolls who were big names in those days, such as Charlie McCarthy, Mortimer Snerd, Knucklehead Smiff and Danny O'Day. All were simple reproductions of the colorful wooden characters that kids and their parents knew from TV and radio. As playthings they were far more than just hot commodities. They were beloved companions.

I got my very own Danny O'Day doll back in 1966, when I was six. That Sears Roebuck version of the TV original was soon my best friend. He came with an instructional record titled *Jimmy Nelson's Instant Ventriloquism and Ventriloquism for the Beginner—the Quickest Course in How to Become a Ventriloquist Ever Devised!* Many an afternoon I sat in front of my big sister's mirror with Danny on my knee, the lessons that emanated from her hi-fi tutoring me on the fundamentals of the art. He would become my all-time favorite toy—the one I carried everywhere, brought to Show-and-Tell and slept with on stormy nights.

Now, it should be made clear here that I never became a ventriloquist—or "vent," as they call themselves. Instead, as I got older, my interests shifted toward another popular way of bringing man-made objects to life; I made a career as an artist in the animated film industry. Ironically for me, around the same time I got my Danny doll, TV cartoons were playing a principal role in ventriloquism's retreat from mainstream entertainment. Could it be that writing this book is my own way of somehow

making up for the 'toon takeover that helped to make dummies disappear from the lime-light? Maybe so, but the simple fact is that I have remained fascinated with an art form that helped define my childhood—my own personal Dummy Days.

Throughout the heyday of radio and into the pioneering days of early television, a Golden Age of ventriloquism occurred in America. Beginning with Edgar Bergen and Charlie McCarthy's radio program in the late 1930s, ventrilo-quism entered the world of popular entertainment with unprecedented appeal and remained in the public eye (and ear) until the mid 1960s. In this era some of the biggest personalities were made of wood, and though these smart-aleck dummies seem to have all but disappeared over the decades, their legacy of wisecracks and sidesplitting fun continues to live on.

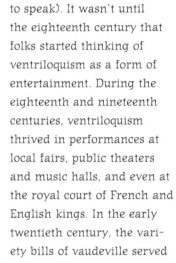

Of course, ventriloquism existed long before radio waves brought voices into homes. The mystics of ancient Egypt conjured up the voices of the gods as proof of their power, and in medieval times ventriloquists stood a good chance of being burned at the stake. It was thought that the ventriloquist's mysterious other voices came from somewhere deep within the gut and probably via unholy rituals. The term, derived from its Latin roots, literally means "belly speaking" (*ventri*, the belly and *loqui*, to speak). It wasn't until the eighteenth century that folks started thinking of ventriloquism as a form of entertainment. During the eighteenth and nineteenth centuries, ventriloquism thrived in performances at local fairs, public theaters and music halls, and even at the royal court of French and English kings. In the early twentieth century, the vari-ety bills of vaudeville served as the perfect venue for ventriloquism acts, and many vents became well-known performers.

Then and now, ventriloquists have been the masters of vocal illusion. They don't actual-ly "throw" their voices, of course, but audiences sure want to believe they do. A technique called the distant voice is very convincing—the vent muffles the second voice, making it sound as if it is coming from a different location. With a figure on his knee, the ventriloquist creates a vocal sleight of hand; the figure is just a decoy, a stage prop that distracts the audience's

11

attention while the vent speaks without moving his or her own lips. Contrary to popular belief, a variety of factors matter in pulling this trick off successfully; it's not just lip control, as I found out after weeks of practicing as a kid. Puppet manipulation, timing, and the ability to act all play a big part in the performance, and the most talented vents perform so convincingly that the audience has a tough time remembering the dummy isn't real. Take for instance the case of First Lady Eleanor Roosevelt who, upon meeting Edgar Bergen and Charlie McCarthy for the first time, leaned forward to shake Charlie's hand. Bergen, caught unaware, had to quickly grab the dummy's wooden hand to meet the First Lady's grip.

In the 1930s when the vaudeville theaters went dark and motion pictures replaced live performances, ventriloquism looked to be a dying art as well. But rather than yield to new trends, the immortal Edgar Bergen single-handedly led a renaissance of ventriloquism by taking the nearly forgotten art form first to nightclubs and film, and then onto the radio. Later, when television eclipsed radio, another

man became instrumental in popularizing ventriloquism: Ed Sullivan, the newspaper columnist-turned-television variety show host. Sullivan's ongoing love for ventriloquists and their dummies led him to regularly invite them onto his long-running show. Often, multiple appearances on Sullivan's show led networks to offer the vents their own TV programs, as was the case for Paul Winchell and Shari Lewis.

Each of the five vents featured in this book appeared on *The Ed Sullivan Show,* and each represents a unique talent with a charm that never wore off. Any regular viewer still remembers Señor Wences, his talking hand Johnny and his echoing head-in-the-box, Pedro. After their introduction on the show, Paul Winchell, Jimmy Nelson and Shari Lewis each took ventriloquism to new heights on TV. Instead of stand-up routines for variety shows, they wrote situation sketches and starred in their own programs or commercials. Winchell and his partner, the red-haired rascal Jerry Mahoney, were to TV viewers in the 1950s what Bergen and Charlie McCarthy were to 1940s radio listeners; theirs was the show both

FLIP CLIP

kids and adults set their clocks by. Because television was still in an experimental stage, Winchell pioneered many technical innovations to "get the dummy off my lap."

Jimmy Nelson made some of the most enduring commercials of the early TV era. Every kid and kid-at-heart in America sang along with Jimmy's droopy-eyed dog Farfel when he spelled success for the chocolate company: "N-E-S-T-L-E-S, Nestle's makes the very best, CHAW-CLAAAAT." The mass-produced dolls based on Nelson's figures, along with instructional albums, inspired and educated many fans in the basics of ventriloquism. Before long, kids like me across the country were sitting with their figure on their knee, looking into mirrors and trying to emulate their hero.

The indefatigable Shari Lewis and her cast of lovable puppets, Lamb Chop, Hush Puppy and Charlie Horse, entered the field of ventriloquism during an era when women were supposed to be at home whipping up Jell-O salads. In the process, this multi-talented performer created an entire show business empire out of a few old socks. From her early appear-ances on Captain Kangaroo to her legendary PBS children's shows in the 1990s, Lewis's career influenced audiences from Baby Boomers to Generation X and beyond.

Alas, in the realm of popular entertain-ment these days, ventrilo-quism seems to have gone the way of plate spinning. In the early days, when spe-cial effects on TV were more difficult to come by, vents held a virtual monopoly on performing on-camera wiz-ardry. Later, when low-cost animation and live-action special effects came along, networks began to make use of new, more sophisticated visual tools and forever changed TV programs for both children and adults. *Ed Sullivan* and those eclectic live vari-ety shows slowly gave way to pre-recorded dramas and sitcoms, and shows like *Bewitched*, *My Favorite Martian*, *The Flintstones* and *The Jetsons* eclipsed the more innocent illusions that ventriloquists offered. Another blow to ventrilo-quism came from the Lenny Bruces of the stand-up comedy world, who laid the ground-work for today's truly "anything-goes" style of entertainment. For the most part, dummies have been left quite speechless in today's world.

It seems that nobody needs Charlie McCarthy to insult celebrities and politicians anymore; there's *Saturday Night Live, South Park* and *The Simpsons* to do the job for him.

To add to the downfall, over the years many movies, books and television shows have created negative stereotypes out of ventriloquists. In films such as *The Dead of the Night* (1945) and *Magic* (1978), vents and their dummies wreak homicidal havoc, propelled by insanity and tortured by psychological demons. Knowledge of ventriloquism is now often portrayed as a quick sign of a twisted mind, and a maniacal dummy is never far behind. Sad to say, people now put ventriloquism in the same category as mind reading and the bearded lady. Let's face it, vents and their partners have gotten the short end of the stick over the years.

And yet, the demise of ventriloquism came not because we fear dummies; it's that society just doesn't need them as much anymore. In the 1950s a ventriloquist's dummy could get away with saying things that people couldn't. In the midst of a repressed culture that feared so much—the bomb, sexuality, communism—Americans relied on ventriloquists to give a voice to the things they were afraid of saying. Perhaps it's another dimension to the verb "to vent"—a wooden dummy could vent desires and concerns that were considered unspeakable. Because the dummy is a unique combination of elements—in stature, a child, and in reality, a fiction (although they certainly seemed real)—those saucy, cheeky boys were able to vocalize feelings and opinions ordinary adults censored.

This is not to say, however, that the mischief-making, all-too-honest sidekick has no place in comedy anymore. Shakespeare's classic fool is still alive and well, a fact I know from my experiences in animated films. The donkey character with Eddie Murphy's vocal chords in the film *Shrek* (2001), for example, is proof positive that the formula of the observant—and often annoying—jokester still works like a charm. Make no mistake about it, there are not as many degrees of separation as one would think between that computer-generated, smooth-talking burro and any of the famous wooden-headed or sock-based talking puppets discussed in this book.

FLIP CLIP

In fact, there are some ventriloquists out there who still manage to secure gigs well within sight of the public spotlight. One such performer is Jeff Dunham (and his insult-slinging, grumpy old partner Walter), who regularly enjoys great exposure on Comedy Central and in leading stand-up comedy clubs nationwide. His brand of outlandish humor—akin to the cantankerous ramblings of Don Rickles or Jackie Mason—always brings down the house and shows no sign of stopping. Dunham, along with a handful of other talented modern-day vents, like Ronn Lucas with his dragon-pal Scorch or Dan Horn and his feisty geriatric Orson, headline major show-rooms in places like Las Vegas and Branson, Missouri. They represent more than mere throwbacks to a bygone era and are living proof that a comic with a dummy can play in the big leagues even now. I like to believe they represent the future of this art.

Born in 1960, I caught the tail end of an era when vents and their dummies were every-where on TV. My Danny O'Day doll remained a fixture in my bedroom, for a while decorating the center of my pillows, then the top of my bookshelf, and finally, after my departure to a faraway art school, the bottom of the cardboard box where he would remain packed away for decades. Today he rests in a glass cabinet, along with several other figures I've collected over the years. You see, I was lucky enough to have been alive at a time when ventriloquists and their dummies were applauded into the spotlight. I lived through some of those glorious Dummy Days. And I miss them.

This book returns to a bygone era in American entertainment. I celebrate Bergen, Lewis, Nelson, Wences and Winchell for bring-ing us characters that came to life. They were part of my childhood and I hope they were part of yours; if not, I hope by the time you have finished this book that you will wish they were. Ventriloquists and their dummies endure as icons of an art form, but more than that, they've become a part of our families and our history.

—KELLY ASBURY

Dummy Days author Kelly Asbury in 2003 with one of the many dummies from his personal collection, an authorized replica of Paul Winchell's Jerry Mahoney.

BERGEN: *Now Charlie, is it true you didn't attend school yesterday?*

CHARLIE: *Well, now Bergen, I . . . well . . . I . . .*

BERGEN: *Young man, I want the full story.*

CHARLIE: *Oh, all right, I'll give you the short version.*

BERGEN: *Charlie, now tell me the truth.*

CHARLIE: *Oh, well, that'll be the long version.*

FLIP CLIP

edgar bergen

Flip Clip

Throughout the 1930s and 1940s, the Effanbee Doll Co. produced miniature toy replicas of Charlie McCarthy, in all his many guises. In this early 1940s photo, taken at Bergen's Beverly Hills home, the real Charlie poses with a group of his tiny toy clones. Today these dolls, like most McCarthy memorabilia, are highly collectible.

In 1938 there were Charlie McCarthy dolls, Charlie hand puppets, Charlie forks, knives and spoons, Charlie wristwatches and wall clocks, Charlie radios, Charlie rings, Charlie wind-up toys, Charlie posters, Charlie comic and coloring books, Charlie Halloween costumes, Charlie tie-tacks, Charlie cups, bowls and glasses, Charlie fan clubs . . . Charlie McCarthy everything and everywhere.

That Charlie McCarthy was only a wooden-headed ventriloquist's dummy was a fact few Americans acknowledged. Charlie's fans adored him and preferred adhering to the playful ideal that he was indeed a real boy who thought and spoke for himself. Edgar Bergen, Charlie's creator and mouthpiece, was of little consequence; the dummy of the duo was the true star of the show.

Like his friend Walt Disney, Bergen understood the value of merchandising his creation, so he licensed his dummy's image on everything from wrapping paper to egg cups; at one point, Bergen was bringing in $400,000 a year on Charlie products alone. During the 1930s and 1940s, only Mickey Mouse surpassed Charlie McCarthy in mass-market popularity. Unlike Disney's goody-two-shoes mouse, however, Charlie's appeal came from his wisecracking ways. He was a dummy with attitude.

There was little that made Charlie stand out from any other ventriloquist's dummy—until he spoke, that is. Then the difference was clear: his razor-sharp tongue and mastery of the quick quip made other dummies (and humans) sound . . . yes, dumb. Audiences rooted for Charlie, perhaps because he was the kid they all secretly wished to be—impolite, argumentative, and not the least bit intimidated by the adult world around him. The comic duo was both irreverent and endearing, a simple formula that brought down the house:

BERGEN: *Now Charlie, I'm trying to tell you a story.*

CHARLIE: *Well, you needn't try so hard.*

BERGEN: *Young man, I wish you'd allow me to finish.*

CHARLIE: *And I wish you would.*

For more than half a century, from the vaudeville era to the advent of television, Edgar Bergen was the world's most popular ventriloquist. And his most famous performances occurred in the unlikeliest of venues for his art form: on the radio. But in the mid 1930s, radio was *everywhere*; over eighty percent of the population in America had at least one wireless, and

FLIP CLIP

Publicity photos such as this one from the early 1940s nurtured the public's idealized view of Charlie as a real boy. Bergen was an amateur pilot and often flew his own twin-engine plane for both business and pleasure. Stenciled on the plane's tail fin was, of course, a silhouette of Charlie.

millions had them in their cars. Every Sunday night from the years 1937 until 1956, almost one-third of American homes were tuned in to hear Bergen and Charlie McCarthy. They were never disappointed with the snappy comebacks and witty banter, but the concept of a ventriloquist act on the radio seems inexplicable now. Early broadcasting executives at NBC Radio City in Hollywood were also skeptical, but their concerns were abated by the show's quick success. Clearly, Bergen had created a character so alive that no one needed to see if his lips were moving. Audiences "saw" Bergen and McCarthy as extremely entertaining, and that was all they needed.

For the first time in the history of ventriloquism, the art took a non-visual form. If this twist seems surprising today, one only needs to hear a recording of Bergen's act to understand. Because of his strength as a writer and his remarkable acting talent, Bergen was able to craft convincing, well-delineated characters that never existed outside of his imagination. Part of Bergen's genius was that he always cast himself as second banana to his alter ego and allowed Charlie to upstage him;

Bergen appears upset that Charlie might be developing his own act in this photo from the 1940s. The great vent—a confirmed bachelor until 1945—often spent his free time concocting photo shoots like this one at his home.

19

Could it be Charlie's long lost sister? Taken in 1923, this is one of the earliest photographs of Bergen with McCarthy. Laura, the female dummy on Bergen's other knee, would soon disappear from the vent's act forever.

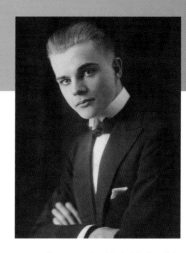

Bergen took pride in his Swedish heritage and could perform his act in Swedish as well as English. This 1923 publicity photo showcases his boyish good looks.

A publicity portrait of Bergen from the 1920s, the decade the vent spent traveling the vaudeville circuit.

if Charlie was brash and opinionated, Bergen was genteel and sophisticated—the quintessential straight man. And comic one-liners, many times ad-libbed, were a Bergen specialty. Perhaps Bergen's greatest strength was his ability to appeal to both adults and children, a skill he honed early in life.

Even when he was a child, the vaudeville stage beckoned to young Edgar John Berggren, the second child of Swedish immigrants Nell and John Berggren. Born February 16, 1903, on their Decatur, Michigan, dairy farm, Bergen's earliest memories were of himself and his older brother Clarence racing to finish their chores so they could catch the latest traveling tent show. The boys sat entranced as jugglers,

animal acts, dancers and acrobats achieved the impossible in front of their eyes. But young Edgar liked the magicians best—those vagabond wizards could produce a live rabbit from thin air, or saw a woman in half and put her back together without a stitch.

This fascination led him to save his pennies and send away for *The Wizard's Manual*, a mail order booklet which included instructions in all manner of illusionary effects that could be achieved at home. The least expensive, and so the most often-tried trick in the book, was referred to as "throwing the voice." Soon on the farm there were strange sounds that seemed to be emanating from cupboards, closets, pickle jars, pies, teapots and pigpens. The boy who wanted to be a magician had inadvertently become a practitioner of that art's less-respected cousin: Edgar Berggren was a ventriloquist. By age thirteen Edgar regularly appeared in school and

FLIP=CLIP

local talent shows with a box of makeshift magic tricks and a homemade papier-mâché dummy.

As he developed his performance skills, the young vent learned to observe the world around him and the real-life characters in it—most notably a red-headed Irish lad who sold papers on a Decatur street corner. The brash newsboy impressed Edgar so much that he drew rough sketches of the kid in the margins of his schoolbooks. These doodles would later prove to be Bergen's most important inspiration.

When Edgar was just sixteen, his father died. Soon thereafter his mother sold the farm and moved with her boys to Chicago. There Edgar took a part-time job in a silent-movie theater, saving whatever small amount of money he could manage. All the while, he continued to perform magic and ventriloquism in amateur shows around town. In April 1922 Berggren realized that a working vent needed a convincing dummy, not the papier-mâché version he'd been using. After asking around town, he found Theodore Mack and Son, a company that sidelined in several entrepreneurial endeavors such as running a small pub and, most importantly, making standard Punch-and-Judy style hand puppets and ventriloquists' dummies. Young Edgar commissioned Mack, a part-time barkeep and furniture maker, to create a more professional-looking figure. Little did Mack or Edgar know how much this new dummy would change their lives and impact entertainment history.

The simple and often-told story of Charlie's beginnings is that Edgar presented

Mack the sketches he had made of the newsboy from Decatur. As is the case with many Hollywood legends, however, this one has its share of controversy. Some versions of the tale claim that the dummy also got its name from the young paperboy, while others believe Charlie's first and last monikers to be derived from Mack's son, Charles. Another source of endless argument concerns the person who actually made Charlie (for more on this, see page 100). The figure was carved from pine and its head outfitted onto the end of a wooden "control stick" which was then fitted into the collar of a hollow mini-torso. The earliest incarnation of the dummy had red hair and wore a sweater, stocking cap, knickers and saddle shoes. And so, for the small sum of thirty-five dollars, Charlie McCarthy was created and a legendary comedy team was born.

With his new dummy, the high school senior secured his first paying engagement— five dollars a night at a semi-professional show in Chicago. For this gig, Berggren decided to drop the magic portion of his act and performed only with Charlie, since it was clear to him that his wooden counterpart was the real crowd pleaser. In fact, later in his life, Bergen credited Charlie with getting him through school. One history teacher passed him solely after witnessing the boy's prodigious talents at a school pageant. "The world needs laughter more than it needs another history teacher," the vent recalled his teacher saying.

After the success of his solo show with Charlie, the young ventriloquist was determined

Bergen wrote, produced, directed and starred as multiple characters in a silent one-reel film called *The Lovin' Swede*. Unfortunately, the short (which Bergen funded himself) was never released. These publicity stills from the film, made sometime in the mid 1920s, depict a rarely seen side of Bergen, who undertook a more serious, straight-man role in his vent acts.

Given the loving father image Bergen cultivated— as evidenced in this publicity shot from 1950— it's hard to know if Charlie's abduction over a decade earlier had been just another PR stunt. Frank Farrell, a reporter for the *World-Telegram*, stole McCarthy from Bergen's Waldorf-Astoria hotel room in March of 1939. The dummy was quickly returned and newspapers across the nation reported the incident as a "kidnapping" rather than an ordinary theft.

to become a professional performer as soon as possible. Edgar shortened his last name, billing himself as "Edgar Bergen—Voice Illusionist," and struck out on vaudeville's so-called Sawdust Trail, a humble circuit of small-town theater and tent shows throughout the Midwest. He booked himself for shows whenever and wherever he could, and by the summer of 1922 the Michigan farm boy was a full-fledged vaudevillian.

When Bergen and McCarthy took to the stage, no one was safe. Charlie's jibes were not only directed at Bergen, but other performers as well. Be they jugglers, acrobats or dancers, no act was immune to Charlie's barbs. To a hapless tenor: "Why, I've known sewing machines who were better 'Singers' than that!" Or perhaps to an earnest contortionist: "Yeah, but can you do this?" followed by a 360-degree spin of his wooden head. Charlie was a hoot on the vaudeville stage, and everyone, even the audience, was fair game.

Summer ended and Bergen entered Chicago's Northwestern University. He paid his tuition from the proceeds of continued performances with Charlie. While his mother hoped he would one day be a doctor, Bergen had other plans. He soon left Northwestern for vaudeville's Chautauqua Circuit. Unlike the Sawdust Trail, the Chautauqua was big time; it had been the starting ground for greats such as the tap-dancing Nicholas Brothers and comedienne Fanny Brice. The Chautauqua included big city theaters not only in the Midwest, but along the eastern seaboard as well. For Bergen, it represented a giant step up. For the next decade, billed as "Bergen and McCarthy," the duo made

the rounds playing every theater that would invite them. During this formative period, Bergen learned the ropes of show business, figuring out which jokes worked and which ones didn't—what got belly laughs in bawdy downtown Chicago or Cincinnati might not play as well with rural crowds in Waterloo, Iowa, or Muncie, Indiana. It was invaluable on-the-job training from which Bergen gleaned his eventual mastery of showmanship.

During its heyday, New York's Palace Theater was the Destination of Dreams, vaude-

Even in still photographs, Bergen displayed an uncanny ability for subtlety in posing and manipulating his dummies. The original wooden version of Charlie, pictured here, had stationary eyes and a mobile mouth and head. Still, Charlie seems alive.

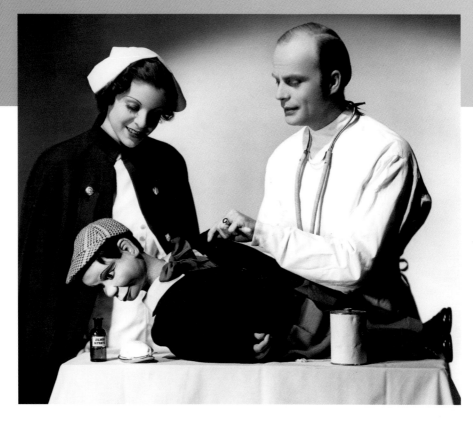

FLIP-CLIP

Bergen and McCarthy, with an unidentified actress, recreate a scene from *The Operation* (1930) for publicity photographs in the 1930s.

ville's Mecca. Entertainment giants such as Harry Houdini, Al Jolson, Fanny Brice and the Marx Brothers performed at the Palace. And, in 1930, Bergen and McCarthy became the Palace's first ventriloquist act. Not only had Edgar Bergen risen to vaudeville's highest plateau, but in terms of legitimacy, he had elevated his chosen art form as well.

Around the same time he first performed at the Palace, Bergen was offered the opportunity to star in several one-reel films produced by the Vitaphone Corp., a subsidiary of Warner Brothers. These short motion pictures screened in vaudeville and movie theaters around the country, shown back-to-back with other shorts or between live acts. The films Bergen made between 1930 and 1937 consist mainly of his more popular sketches from his repertoire at the time. Fortunately for vent fans, the first short he made depicts the duo performing "The Operation," in which Charlie is cast as a boy in need of a tonsillectomy and Bergen is the harried doctor. The skit was so hilarious that Bergen went on to perform it around the world for years to come:

BERGEN: *Now listen, young man, it's not going to hurt you at all and if it does, I'll give you an anesthetic.*

CHARLIE: *Yeah?*

BERGEN: *Yes.*

CHARLIE: *A 'stetic, huh?*

BERGEN: *Yes, an anesthetic.*

CHARLIE: *Well, what's a 'stetic?*

BERGEN: *Well, there are several kinds.*

CHARLIE: *Well, drag 'em out.*

BERGEN: *All right, uh, there's chloroform, ether, gas and a local.*

CHARLIE: *Uh huh, nice menu.*

BERGEN: *Yes, it is. Now, what would you like?*

CHARLIE: *I'll take vanilla!*

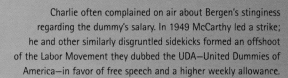

Charlie often complained on air about Bergen's stinginess regarding the dummy's salary. In 1949 McCarthy led a strike; he and other similarly disgruntled sidekicks formed an offshoot of the Labor Movement they dubbed the UDA—United Dummies of America—in favor of free speech and a higher weekly allowance.

In 1936 when Bergen retooled Charlie's appearance to better suit America's debonair supper club crowd, he not only changed the face of his dummy, but also the art of ventriloquism. This creative photograph served as an advertisement for the revamped act and alerted nightclub patrons that there was a new dummy on the block.

It's astonishing to watch Bergen moving with such confidence and dexterity, especially given his youth and limited experience. He is able to manipulate Charlie's mouth and body with one hand while applying a stethoscope and listening to Charlie's chest with the other hand. The choreography is so convincing that Charlie comes to life in the scene. As he makes passes at a young nurse, talks incessantly, and flusters the hapless Dr. Bergen, it's hard to believe the ornery boy is just a dummy. Also evident in the film is Bergen's strong lip control, a skill he would later admit was weakened by his subsequent years on the radio.

But soon feature-length motion pictures would transform the entertainment world and leave Bergen, like so many other performers, looking for work. The advent of full-length "talkies" and the popularity of radio were the fatal blows to vaudeville. When the great Palace went dark in 1932, so, too, did vaudeville. By 1933 Edgar Bergen was all but out of work. In her 1984 memoir *Knock Wood,* Candice Bergen recalls her father describing this difficult time: "'Everybody looked down on ventriloquism. Vaudeville was dying . . . We thought we were through, Charlie and I.'"

Always the innovator, Edgar Bergen came up with an idea that would soon create an entirely new livelihood for ventriloquists: the nightclub circuit. But some changes needed to be made in his act first. Big city nightclubs and supper clubs were strictly adult venues, which possessed an air of sophistication vaudeville most certainly lacked.

Bergen, a keen social observer, considered the day's most accurate meter of the debonair to be *Esquire* magazine, which featured its mustachioed mascot Esky in a tuxedo, top hat and monocle. Bergen's original idea was to acquire permission from the magazine to create a new dummy in Esky's likeness. The deal almost went through when fate stepped in—on Charlie's behalf—and *Esquire*'s lawyers added licensing fees to the contract. Rather than taking on any new business partners, Edgar came up with another approach: *Esquire* may have owned the rights to Esky, but that didn't mean Charlie couldn't dress like him. Hence, in early 1936, Charlie underwent a considerable makeover, and another pop culture icon was born, almost as an afterthought.

Charlie's new appearance did not catch on right away in the tough new nightclub circuit. Bergen, also wearing formal attire, found himself playing late-night engagements at second-rate joints where a tie and tails were decidedly out of place. But he and Charlie persevered, finally making their way out of the dive bars and into an extended run at Chicago's Chez Paree nightclub. Here Bergen would receive the first of many small breaks—an invitation to appear at a high-society party.

FLIP-CLIP

Radio star Rudy Vallee was also an accomplished amateur ventriloquist and lifelong enthusiast of the art.

It just so happened that Noel Coward, the esteemed playwright and society man, was a guest at the party. He was so impressed by Bergen's act that he assisted the vent in securing an important gig at the Rainbow Room in Manhattan. There the crowd adored Bergen and McCarthy, and by late 1936 the ventriloquist was regularly entertaining New York's elite society crowd.

But Bergen's biggest break came when the well-connected Coward helped him appear on the popular radio program *The Fleischmann Hour* (named for its sponsor, the yeast supplier). Rudy Vallee, a predecessor to the likes of crooners such as Bing Crosby and Frank Sinatra, hosted the popular NBC variety show, which broadcast live from Hollywood. Bergen was slated for a spot on the December 17, 1936 show. Though many of the executives at NBC questioned Vallee's choice of a ventriloquist act for the radio waves, Vallee remained undaunted. When asked, "Why a ventriloquist?" Vallee simply retorted, "Why not?" So Americans across the country heard Edgar Bergen and Charlie McCarthy for the first time on Vallee's show. Obviously, the listeners agreed with Vallee— and Bergen's act found a new home.

In 1937, after Bergen and McCarthy had finished an extended three-month run on Vallee's show, NBC offered Edgar Bergen his own live radio show. Officially known as *The Chase and Sanborn Hour* for its sponsor, a well-known coffee

Bergen and McCarthy starred with Lucille Ball in the 1941 film *Look Who's Laughing!* Based on the popular radio program *Fibber McGee and Molly*, the film was the most profitable feature that year for its producing studio RKO. Lucy plays Julie Patterson, Bergen's love interest, and as always Charlie gets right in the middle of things:

BALL:
Marriage is a strong institution, Charlie.

CHARLIE:
So is Alcatraz, but I wouldn't want to live there.

company, audiences began to simply call the program "The Charlie McCarthy Show." Bergen's fame had once again been eclipsed by his creation, but he had no reason to complain; success had brought him prosperity. As his program thrived, he and his mother relocated from New York to Beverly Hills, purchasing a beautiful hilltop home he dubbed "Bella Vista."

The new show was an instant hit. It quickly became the fashion among celebrities to guest star on it, and no matter how famous they were, they would all be in for a spate of Charlie's merciless ribbing. Indeed, the wisecracking style that had served Edgar Bergen so well from his earliest days on stage worked more reliably than ever on radio. For the run of the program, the stars delighted in meeting Charlie McCarthy—with one celebrated exception.

W.C. Fields was Charlie's arch nemesis. World-famous as a vaudeville and film performer, Fields played the classic curmudgeon: a constantly frustrated, work-avoiding dipsomaniac and hater of dogs, mothers-in-law and especially children (even wooden ones). Charlie was his perfect foil,

Charlie McCarthy and W.C Fields worked together throughout the 1930s and 1940s—even though they hated one another. In this photo from *You Can't Cheat an Honest Man* (1939), carnival huckster Fields introduces "The Great Edgar." Charlie's beautiful swami garb, pictured here, is indicative of the many elaborate costumes the dummy wore in Hollywood films.

and whenever Fields guest starred on the show, their verbal feuds were inevitable:

FIELDS:
Ah, if it isn't young Charles McCarthy, the woodpecker's pin-up boy.

CHARLIE:
Ah, Mr. Fields, when I see that nose of yours, I'm reminded of the lighthouse on Cape Cod.

FIELDS:
Speaking of noses, don't you ever sneeze around me, McCarthy.
I'll get sawdust in my eyes.

CHARLIE:
If your nose gets anywhere near loose sawdust, there'll be an explosion.

FLIP ⚡ CLIP

FIELDS: Why you little blockhead,
            I'll whittle you down to a
            coat hanger.

CHARLIE: I'll stick a wick in your mouth
            and use you for an oil lamp.

FIELDS: Ah, such a charming young lad.
            Children are such a joy. Why,
            I'm reminded of the time when I,
            on my own unsteady legs, would
            toddle from room to room.

CHARLIE: When was that . . . last night?

Fields and McCarthy's rivalry delighted radio listeners; the duo's quarrelling was charismatic and convincing. In fact, in her memoir, Candice Bergen states that it wasn't just an act—the great comedian actually did hate the dummy.

Next to Fields, Bergen and McCarthy's most famous—and infamous—guest was Mae West, whose appearance on December 12, 1937 scandalized listeners and made headlines. A skit that featured West as a vampish version of Eve prompted the Federal Communications Commission's condemnation of the show and its parent network, NBC. As if the blasphemous subject matter weren't enough, Bergen and West pushed the boundaries even further with the following line:

WEST: (to Charlie) Why don't you
        come on home with me, Honey?
        I'll let you play in my woodpile.

In an era when the Hays Office and the Legion of Decency set moral codes for the motion picture industry, the entire entertainment world was under constant self-scrutiny for "objectionable" programming. NBC issued a formal public apology and ceremoniously banned Mae West from its network for the next fifteen years. Immediately after the controversy, *The Chase and Sanborn Hour* reportedly experienced an enormous jump in ratings. The bad publicity only proved that Charlie McCarthy's mouth was indomitable. Adults loved that Bergen and McCarthy could poke fun at the cultural mores of the day in such a lighthearted way.

Bergen went to zany lengths to make Charlie seem real. The wooden figure had his own furnished bedroom and bath at the Bergen house, complete with tub and toothbrush. Many articles about Charlie appeared in magazines, including an entire publication called *A Day with Charlie McCarthy* which featured him in the midst of daily activities such as brushing his teeth and breakfasting with his "dad" Bergen. These puff publicity pieces worked, and people treated Charlie like a real boy; the dummy received thousands of fan letters weekly. Pinocchio would have been green with envy.

Edgar Bergen's desire that Charlie be perceived as flesh and blood was satisfied in 1938, when his dummy partner's hand and footprints joined those of other Hollywood legends in the forecourt of Grauman's Chinese Theatre.

Again like Walt Disney, Bergen recognized the importance of adding new inhabitants to his stable of characters, though none would ever surpass Charlie McCarthy in popularity. In 1936 the dim-witted country bumpkin Mortimer Snerd joined the act. Sculpted by puppet maker Virginia Austin Curtis, supposedly from sketches drawn by Bergen, the cartoonish new figure was a three-dimensional stereotype of ignorance: droopily crossed eyes, pronounced overbite, vacuous grin, unkempt bushy hair, wilted straw hat and loud bow tie. "Scientifically stupid," was how Bergen once described him, and Mortimer did not disappoint:

Over the course of his nineteen years on radio, Bergen hosted many celebrity guests. This 1950s publicity shot features Bergen and Charlie, costumed as a swami and a Foreign Legionnaire respectively, with James Cagney (left) and Ronald Reagan.

BERGEN: *Please, tell us your name.*

MORTIMER: *Uh . . . well, it's uh . . .
            ah, shucks, I know it like my
            own name.*

BERGEN: *It's Mortimer . . .
            Mortimer Snerd.*

MORTIMER: *You don't say (yuck, yuck)?*

BERGEN: *Oh, Mortimer, how did you get
            to be so stupid?*

MORTIMER: *Ah, just lucky I guess
            (yuck, yuck).*

Adding another character to his show presented a challenge to Bergen, however. He knew well that his live audience would be disappointed to see one drooping dummy waiting to be brought to life while the other was on his knee, so he had to improvise new performing techniques. Bergen made certain that when Charlie and Mortimer were both in view, they were either talking to him or to each other in rapid-fire succession. Although no easy task for a ventriloquist, Bergen the virtuoso performer pulled though.

In 1944 Bergen added a female dummy to the group. Effie Klinker, a smart-looking, bespectacled spinster, was reportedly modeled after a country schoolteacher he once admired. She too delighted audiences with off-color remarks that were totally inconsistent with her straight-laced appearance. Bergen often brought her out to help warm-up his studio audience and occasionally used her in his program. Her lines were always endearingly tartish:

Frustrated spinster Effie Klinker asks Bergen to "conjure me a man." Created in 1944, Effie served as an outlet for Bergen's bawdy side—as evidenced in a rare tape recording of a live performance with the character that reveals the vent using language forbidden on radio and TV.

EFFIE.   *If a man gets fresh with me,*
            I usually tell him a thing or two.

BERGEN: *What's that?*

EFFIE: *My address and phone number.*

Bergen's brand of humor, innocence and sincerity, spiced with more than a hint of innuendo, was in keeping with the popular taste of the time. Other radio shows and comic films of the period, like the much-loved *Fibber McGee and Molly* program or the *Ma and Pa Kettle* movie series, reveal similar sensibilities. Edgar Bergen was more than just a fringe offshoot of pop culture; his characters helped define an era in entertainment history. From his earliest radio success on, Bergen was the ventriloquist against whom all others were measured, if not for technique, then for his mastery of comic characterizations and showmanship. Later

Frances Bergen takes to the wheel of the family's antique Tin Lizzie, which was often used for publicity photos like this one from 1949. Three-year-old Candice is seated next to Charlie, as Effie and Mortimer flank Podine Puffington and a rather flirtatious looking Edgar.

from the one who knew him best

Edgar Bergen could be self-deprecating and often called himself "a terrible ventriloquist." He would never have admitted to the fact that he was simply a great entertainer. But that is, happily, how I hope he will always be remembered.

Edgar was also complex, multitalented and wonderfully eccentric. He was shy, and though he sometimes found it difficult to open up emotionally, his spontaneous sense of humor was best expressed through his characters . . .

like Charlie McCarthy . . .

BERGEN: *I just forgot what I was going*
          to say.

CHARLIE: *You want to sit on my lap?*

BERGEN: *You know that gravity was*
          discovered by a man named
          Issac Newton.

CHARLIE: *Did he have a brother*
          named Fig?

and Mortimer Snerd . . .

BERGEN: *Now when you go to court with*
           your grandpa, Mortimer, when
           the judge enters, you stand up.

MORTIMER: *Why? Have I got his seat?*

BERGEN: *The judge wears a long*
           black robe that shows his
           authority.

MORTIMER: *You mean it ain't long enough?*

—FRANCES BERGEN

Flip Clip

One of Bergen's most memorable radio stunts was Charlie's mock engagement to Marilyn Monroe in the early 1950s. Though preparation for the marriage stretched over three consecutive weeks, the comic union never came to pass. It seems that, when asked to take the required blood test for a marriage license, Charlie was unable to deliver.

Used primarily for his television appearance, life-sized Podine Puffington was created by Bergen around 1950. It was no coincidence that the pretty, southern belle puppet came from, as she said it, "Al'bama." Bergen's wife, Frances, was born and raised in Montgomery.

ventriloquists such as Paul Winchell, Jimmy Nelson and Shari Lewis, as well as the legendary Muppeteer Jim Henson, openly credited Bergen as their vent hero.

Bergen's talent for performing was not lost on the Hollywood film community. During his early radio days, he and his characters appeared in several feature-length films, such as *The Goldwyn Follies* (1938), *Charlie McCarthy, Detective* (1939) and most notably *You Can't Cheat an Honest Man* (1939) with W.C. Fields. And his film performances were not limited to ventriloquism. Bergen had attempted some Chaplin-esque short films during the silent film era based on a tramp character he created called "The Lovin' Swede." Only a single one-reeler was ever completed ("I filmed my own screen test to take to Hollywood . . . and Hollywood let me take it back home," Bergen commented), but he never lost his thespian ambitions. In 1947 he was cast as the elderly Mr. Thorkelson in the feature film *I Remember Mama*, which also starred Irene Dunne in an Oscar-winning performance. Bergen would always remember that experience with pride, perhaps as proof that he could succeed without a dummy on his knee.

Edgar Bergen's films with Charlie offer a rare, first-hand glimpse of a master ventriloquist at work, and they are valuable resources even for today's vents. A quirky detail in these films is the way moviemakers treated the vent/dummy partnership; in some scenes Charlie is clearly acknowledged as a puppet in need of his manipulator's voice, while in others he interacts with humans all by himself. Despite oddities in having his talents adapted to the silver screen, Bergen's level of fame was enough to keep the film studios knocking at his door.

The movie folk appreciated his efforts enough to award Edgar Bergen with their industry's highest honor in 1937—a miniature, wooden Academy Award with a slotted, movable mouth—for his "Outstanding Comic Creation" of Charlie McCarthy. Today, Bergen's Oscar is permanently on display in Chicago's Museum of Broadcast Communications. The prosperous and creative

Only W.C. Fields was billed above Bergen and McCarthy for *You Can't Cheat an Honest Man* on this lobby card for the film. It is interesting to note in the artwork that, while McCarthy and Fields get the broad cartoon treatment, Bergen is depicted with more restraint—the straight man even in caricature.

years that followed this award brought other honors—but not for Bergen. Ironically, Charlie took all the honors, including Grand Marshall of Pasadena's annual Tournament of Roses, "Mayor for a Day" in San Francisco and an honorary "Master of Innuendo and Snappy Comebacks" degree from Northwestern University, the school Bergen had attended.

Bergen was one of the first entertainers to put on wartime shows for servicemen. During World War II, Bergen and McCarthy entertained the troops both at home and abroad, alongside the likes of Bob Hope, Martha Rae, Betty Grable and the Andrews Sisters. The boy from Decatur, lover of the traveling tent show, was now a member of the noblest brand of vagabond performer. The USO was vaudeville with a cause.

The world was changing fast, and on the home front, Bergen's personal life was evolving as well. In June 1945, not long after his mother's death, the forty-year-old Bergen married a

twenty-year-old fashion model named Frances Westerman. The couple had met at one of his nightclub shows. "I had gone to the show with a friend of mine who worked with Edgar," Frances Bergen remembers. "He spotted me in the audience and bashfully asked her 'who was that girl with the long legs?' Well, not long after that we started dating and about a year later got married." On May 9, 1946 the couple had their first child, a little girl they named Candice. Charlie had gained a baby sister.

When Bergen's contract with NBC ended in 1948, CBS quickly signed the popular ventriloquist for a show. Sponsored by Coca-Cola, *The New Edgar Bergen Hour* presented the same tried-

Bergen and McCarthy received their special wooden Oscar in March 1938, within a year of the duo's initial success on the radio. Charlie's popularity quickly won over the members of the Academy, though he had only appeared in two feature-length films by that time. In this photograph taken in the late 1960s, the vent partners reminisce about the occasion.

In 1949 Bergen began a new radio program sponsored by the Coca-Cola Co. *The Edgar Bergen Show with Charlie McCarthy* remained on the air until 1956. Colorful ads featuring the famous vent duo with the popular soft drink became a common part of America's commercial graphics landscape, appearing in magazines, train stations, movie lobbies and on billboards.

This "Elderly Charlie" from the mid 1950s actually started out as a "Sleepy Charlie" dummy which had been made during the 1940s for use in movies. At least two Bergen-commissioned sleepy-eyed versions are known to have existed and are owned by private collectors.

whatever happened to charlie and the gang?

Try as he did to convince the world that Charlie McCarthy was almost human, at times Edgar Bergen had to face the reality that the dummy was, after all, just a dummy. Things could go wrong with that miniature body and its wooden head: springs could break, face paint could chip, hinges could wear out. For such times, it was critical that Bergen have a backup figure, an exact double that would let the show go on without anyone the wiser. In addition, if Bergen wanted Charlie's eyes to move or his expression to look sleepy or sad, a special version of the dummy then had to be made.

Because Bergen kept no official records of how many Charlies were produced for him in his fifty-six-year career, no one today knows the exact number of authorized Charlie McCarthy dummies in existence. All educated estimates—from historians and collectors alike—conclude that Bergen commissioned at least thirteen of them to serve different purposes in his act, including several backup versions. Any version that Bergen commissioned for such use is regarded as an original by aficionados.

To modern-day collectors, these authentic Charlies are highly prized. Ever since Bergen's death in 1978, fans, collectors and pop culture history buffs have tried to keep careful track of their whereabouts. Most notable among these experts is voice actor Doug Preis, whose professional repertoire includes uncannily accurate impersonations of all of Bergen's voices. Preis is also a vintage puppet collector, and—most significantly here—he has been officially designated by the Bergen family as creative consultant, historian and archivist for the Bergen Foundation. Preis works diligently to follow the fate of all the

Charlies and all of the original versions of other Bergen characters. "My primary goal," Preis says, "is to help preserve, protect and perpetuate the art and magic of Edgar Bergen." He owns the largest known private collection of Bergen and McCarthy memorabilia, including vintage toys, radios, books and games, as well as many of the specially made costumes used for Charlie in Bergen's Hollywood films. Among these, displayed on a perfect, custom-made collector's replica of the famous dummy, is the Sherlock Holmes-like cape and cap from the 1939 movie *Charlie McCarthy, Detective.*

With Preis's help, the Bergen family continually attempts to account for all of the versions of Charlie McCarthy that Bergen used in his career. Identifying an original Charlie for Preis means undertaking an almost forensic investigation, comparing old photos and frames of movie film in order to look for variations in certain features on the puppets. This is complicated by the fact that, while Chicago furniture makers Theodore Mack and Son indeed made the very first 1922 version of Charlie for Bergen, other craftsmen are believed to have produced many of the doubles. Puppet makers like Alex Cameron, who purchased Mack's shop in 1925, Frank Marshall, who subsequently took it over from Cameron in 1927, and Robert Wallace, who is said to have created puppets for Bergen during the 1940s, have long been associated with the later Charlies, though none can be positively attributed to them. It seems that none of the figure makers left any distinguishing marks, an unfortunate fact which has led to the ongoing mystery among collectors: Whatever happened to all of Bergen's authorized Charlies?

The earliest Charlie used in the first Vitaphone shorts clearly has stationary eyes, while other clips from the same series show eyes that move. The 1939 feature *You Can't Cheat an Honest Man* proves that some of the Charlie figures not only had moving eyes, but a variety of facial expressions as well. There was at least one angry, frowning Charlie and also a sleepy-eyed Charlie that was later retooled into an elderly Charlie. A very early version of Charlie—with moving eyes—is on display at the Smithsonian Institution. Fiberglass versions of Charlie and Effie Klinker, along with an early version of Mortimer Snerd, are currently on display at Chicago's Museum of Broadcast Communications. One of the first authorized versions of Bergen's famed dummy, often used in feature films and known as the "Movie Charlie," was sold at auction in 1995 for the reported sum of $100,000 to popular magician David Copperfield. (Himself a former vent, Copperfield is said to also own a sleepy-eyed version of Charlie.) At least three Charlies are rumored to have been destroyed during Bergen's lifetime, for reasons unknown. The remaining figures reside in private collections or are still in the possession of the Bergen family. Every now and then another "Charlie" crops up, Preis acknowledges. But the exact number of originals floating around outside the collector community is unknown. Perhaps, locked away in an old trunk backstage at some dilapidated vaudeville theater or buried amid the forgotten relics of some collector's attic, there's a perfectly preserved backup of Charlie McCarthy waiting patiently to be discovered. Charlie will undoubtedly be the subject of a never-ending treasure hunt.

During a tour of Hawaii in the mid 1940s Bergen seized the opportunity for a few Polynesian-influenced publicity shots of Charlie and Mortimer Snerd. One can hope that's only coconut milk they're drinking.

Charlie teasingly ad-libbed after one Bergen flub, "On TV, you have to memorize the lines!"

Puppetry and ventriloquism would become staples on American television screens during this decade. Professionals such as Paul Winchell with his dummy Jerry Mahoney and Shari Lewis with her sock puppet Lamb Chop were among a handful of ventriloquists who enjoyed major success hosting their own network shows in the 1950s. Though Edgar Bergen's influence on all such performers was openly evident, history's most famous ventriloquist never found a permanent home in TV-land. One could speculate about reasons for this, although the most cited explanation is Bergen's increasingly evident lip movement, which had worsened due to decades spent on

and-true format as Bergen's former show and even ran in the same Sunday night time slot. Wherever Bergen and McCarthy went, so did most of their audience, and the duo continued to enjoy enormous popularity on their new network.

Then the entire entertainment world—and American culture—changed. The 1950s rolled around, and with the new decade came a new fascination: television. Radio and film would never be the same again, nor would Edgar Bergen's career. Audiences advanced (or regressed, depending on one's opinion) to watching more TV shows, and though Bergen's radio show would continue airing on Sunday evenings until 1956, the time came to try a TV special. *The Edgar Bergen Show Featuring Charlie McCarthy* aired in the fall of 1950, featuring variety acts as well as sketches with Charlie, Mortimer, Effie and a new, flirtatious southern belle figure known as Podine Puffington. Bergen's talents for funny characterizations were as apparent as ever, his timing only slightly hampered by TV's less forgiving format. As

Probably taken near the time of Effie Klinker's creation in 1944, this photo shows Bergen with his dummies in the garage of his Beverly Hills home. The space often served as a makeshift practice stage and photography studio.

33

Bergen was always self-deprecating about his talents. A *Colliers* magazine article from April 29, 1950 quoted him hilariously venting his feelings about his role: "Groucho Marx can be funny without the dummy brother; Charlie Chaplin doesn't always have to carry his cane and derby hat; W.C. Fields was good for a laugh with or without billiard cue. But who, Bergen asks, is Bergen without Charlie? 'A nobody! How I would love to trade places with Charlie and be as accepted as he is.'"

radio. Or perhaps Bergen's vaudevillian-based, "softer" brand of humor was becoming passé in a world preparing itself for a race to the moon. In any case, Bergen often stated his preference for radio, a format that allowed him more flexibility to conjure up images of exotic locations and innumerable wacky situations. More than likely, television never fully embraced Edgar Bergen because he never fully embraced television.

By the 1960s ventriloquism in general was on the decline. Ventriloquists began to be viewed as relics—throwbacks to earlier, less cosmopolitan days. In much the same way that crooners such as Bing Crosby and Sinatra had given way to the gyrating Elvis in 1956, and again in the early 1960s when a more established Presley had fallen to the "fab" Beatles, the sharp, satirical humor of comedians such as Lenny Bruce began to seem better suited to the era. Times had certainly changed, and somewhere in the midst of all the social and political turmoil, Charlie's naughty innuendoes lost their edge.

Though he would not officially retire for seventeen more years, Edgar Bergen found himself with more time on his hands, and Charlie

spent more nights tucked inside his trunk. While he continued to perform on TV and stage throughout the 1960s and 1970s, Bergen's family began to take top priority. His son Kris Edgar Bergen was born on October 12, 1961. Unlike Candice, who had been raised during the heyday of her father's celebrity, Kris grew up less aware

The tremendous fame of Bergen and McCarthy remains unmatched by any other ventriloquism team. The duo had a lasting influence on the art form, as evidenced in the outpouring of affection at Bergen's funeral. In attendance were pallbearers Milton Berle, Art Linkletter, Ken Murray, Rudy Vallee, Mervin LeRoy, and Freeman Gosden. Jim Henson, with Kermit at his side, spoke of the late vent's genius, as did Ronald Reagan and Johnny Carson, who revealed that it was his admiration of Bergen that led him into showbiz.

of his father's fame. In earlier days when heavy performance schedules dictated that Charlie and the show took center stage, Bergen's domestic life may have suffered. Now the aging ventriloquist could devote himself to his young son and did so with gusto. "When I was growing up, my dad was truly my best friend," Kris Bergen says. "I didn't know him as 'Edgar Bergen the Famous Ventriloquist.' I just knew him as 'Dad.'"

Another source of tremendous pride for Frances and Edgar Bergen was their talented daughter Candice's rise to fame as a fashion model, accomplished photojournalist and actress. Eventually, in the 1990s, Candice Bergen's stardom would equal her father's. Her multi-Emmy-winning role in the television sitcom *Murphy Brown* proved that she had inherited her father's wise-cracking ways.

Bergen's final curtain call was a fitting finale to a most illustrious career. In September 1978 Bergen held a press conference announcing that he would retire from show business after a two-week engagement at Caesar's Palace in Las Vegas. Billed alongside singer Andy Williams, the vent's final Vegas gig played to a full house and proved triumphant as Bergen, Charlie and Mortimer performed

flawlessly. It was a funny, nostalgic experience, "really was the best performance of his life," as noted by wife Frances. Bergen ended his performance with a special farewell: "In vaudeville, every act has to have an opening and a close, and I think, for me, the close has come and it's time to pack up my little friends and say goodbye. Goodnight and thank you all for listening."

On September 30, 1978, just a few hours after this final performance, seventy-five-year-old Edgar Bergen died peacefully in his sleep. Frances—not Charlie—was by his side.

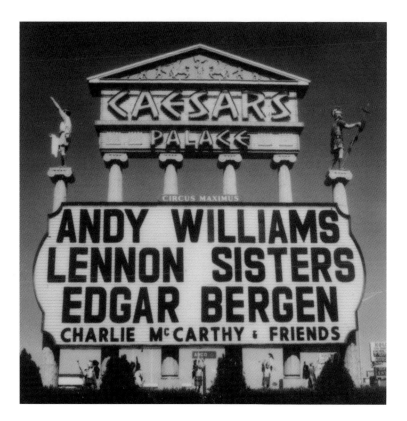

In September of 1978 Bergen and McCarthy enjoyed their final star billing. It was a fitting capper to an amazing career.

NAME: LAURA

ARRIVED ON THE SCENE: early 1920s

DISTINGUISHING CHARACTERISTICS:
her near total obscurity.

Probably created during Bergen's early vaudeville days, little is known about this girl dummy who was never utilized at any other point in Bergen's career. She is pictured, however, alongside Charlie McCarthy in some promotional photographs from the early 1920s. When Bergen realized what a hit Charlie was going to be, he probably opted to end Laura's short-lived career.

NAME: CHARLIE McCARTHY

ARRIVED ON THE SCENE: April 1922,
carved by Theodore Mack and Son

DISTINGUISHING CHARACTERISTICS:
irrepressibility; a top hat and monocle (after 1936); razor-sharp tongue and ever-present wit (always).

The world's most well-known wooden-head, Charlie McCarthy became the dummy every other dummy wanted to be: rich, famous and full of smart remarks. Often made headlines as Candice Bergen's little brother, W.C. Fields's greatest nemesis and Marilyn Monroe's fiancé.

FAMED REMARK: Too numerous to select just one. "I'll clip ya, so help me, I'll mow ya down!" "Hard work never killed anybody, but why take a chance?" "When I get smitten, I stay smut."

NAME: MORTIMER SNERD

ARRIVED ON THE SCENE: 1936,
sculpted by Virginia Austin Curtis

DISTINGUISHING CHARACTERISTICS:
buck teeth, straw hat, relentless stupidity

Charlie's country-bumpkin cousin, who often joined in on Bergen's radio program, Mortimer's popularity would almost rival that of Charlie. Mort was often known to forget his own name. Occasionally referred to as "Professor Snerd."

FAMED REMARK: "Duh . . . I'll go along with that!"

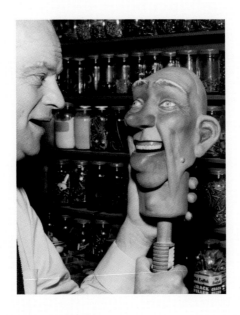

NAME: EFFIE KLINKER

ARRIVED ON THE SCENE: 1944

DISTINGUISHING CHARACTERISTICS:

high-collared blouse, spectacles perched precariously on the end of her nose, flirtatiousness

The man-crazy spinster Effie made many brief but memorable cameo appearances on Bergen's radio show. She also appeared with Bergen, Charlie and Mort in episodes of the TV game show, *Do You Trust Your Wife?*, which Bergen hosted from 1956 to 1958.

FAMED REMARK: "No, I never married . . . No, darn it, no!"

NAME: LARS LUNDQUIST

ARRIVED ON THE SCENE: unknown, photos suggest late 1940s

DISTINGUISHING CHARACTERISTICS:

bald head, big ears, love of lingonberries

Little is known about this character, except that he spoke only Swedish. The bilingual Bergen performed with Lars for special events, including an appearance before Sweden's Royal Family. On that occasion Bergen and Lars were honored with The Royal Order of Vasa and The Order of the North Star conferred by King Gustav V.

FAMED REMARK: sadly, lost in translation

NAME: PODINE PUFFINGTON

AARRIVED ON THE SCENE: in the later years of Bergen's career, mostly for TV

DISTINGUISHING CHARACTERISTICS:

height (Podine was life-sized), southern accent

This southern belle was Bergen's most lifelike dummy. She was blond with a heavily made-up face and had a typical slotted-mouth mechanism attached to a hollow torso. Beneath this flowed a floor-length skirt that concealed the fact that the poor dear was legless. When held correctly by Bergen, the dummy and the vent could dance "cheek to cheek." Podine delighted Bergen's viewing audiences with her sweeping skirts and waltzing ability.

FAMED REMARK: "Ahm frum Al'bama!"

WENCES: *S'awright?*

PEDRO: *S'awright!*

FLIP-CLIP

señor wences

Flip Clip

I f ever there was a surrealist ventriloquist, it was Señor Wences. His act was a case study in the bizarre. For more than eight decades this quirky vent conjured a glorious career from the most unlikely of props, from din- ner plates to a head-in-the-box to a face on his hand. Indeed, Wences's closed fist—glamorized with two doll eyes, a dash of lipstick and a blond wig—formed one of the vent's most enduring creations, Johnny. Standing onstage, Wences would hold up the side of his decorated fist so the audience could see the curled index finger wrapped by his thumb. As he flexed his thumb, a mouth defined by lipstick appeared to form words and little Johnny would come to life:

Boy or girl? The gender of Wences's famous hand puppet has often been disputed. Despite the character's long hair, high-pitched voice and red lips, Johnny was indeed male.

WENCES:	*You sing for us?*
JOHNNY:	*S'okay.*
WENCES:	*(cautious tone)* *Ees dee-fee-cult.*
JOHNNY:	*Ees easy.*
WENCES:	*Dee-fee-cult.*
JOHNNY:	*Easy.*
WENCES:	*Dee-fee-cult!*
JOHNNY:	*Dee-fee-cult for you.* *Easy for me!*

Wences's affinity for imbuing life into found objects (including his hand) began when he was a child. Born in Peñeranda, Spain, on April 17, 1896, Wenceslao Moreno was the fifth child in a family of seventeen children. Already as a young boy, Wenceslao's talent for mimicry and sense of fun were apparent. At a time before mailboxes existed in his apartment house, he would imitate the voice of the mail- man calling all of the tenants down to pick up their mail. They would stop what they were doing at the moment and dutifully gather at the front door, only to find that the mailman wasn't there (one tenant became so angered at this that he reportedly dumped a pail of water over the mailman's head). Wenceslao's practical jokes must have been by turns infectious and infuriating for the Moreno family.

In a publicity photo from the 1940s, Señor Wences scolds the "dee-fee-cult" Johnny.

Backlighting on this 1940s headshot gives Wences the sinister star appeal of a Hollywood character actor. Don't be confused— it isn't Vincent Price.

After his family moved to nearby Salamanca, Wenceslao gained a reputation as the class clown. Often he would imitate his classmates' voices; when one of them was absent, Wenceslao would answer in his place and the teacher would mark the absentee present. Wences legend suggests it was during a prank at school that he discovered an important gimmick, one which would later become his renowned Johnny. As the story goes, one day— probably after another of his disruptive shenanigans—Wenceslao's schoolteacher punished him by ordering him to clean and refill the classroom inkwells. While doing so, Wenceslao noticed that the black ink smeared around his left forefinger and thumb resembled a pair of lips. He added two dots near his upper knuckle and created a face. Holding a loose fist, he began to wiggle his thumb, giving the illusion of a moving mouth—his hand had become a tiny person. Wenceslao then endowed his creation with a high-pitched, funny falsetto. Fellow classmates burst into laughter, and thankfully, so did his teacher. Who knew at the time that from such a modest start, this comic duo would someday travel the world together?

As Natalie "Taly" Cover Moreno, Wences's widow, recalls, "In those days in Spain, a boy really only had three choices for a career: the church, politics or bullfighting."

41

There was little stigma attached to a smoking little boy back in the 1940s. Johnny's ability to blow smoke rings was one of Señor Wences's most unique gimmicks.

At age sixteen Wenceslao chose the latter. Few details are known about his days as a bullfighter, except that the young matador never stopped practicing his other performance skills such as juggling, plate spinning, sleight of hand and ventriloquism.

After a series of close calls in the ring, his bullfighting career ended and Wenceslao Moreno took up stage performing full time. For several years he traveled around Spain, performing a conventional ventriloquist act with a wooden dummy in tent shows and cabarets. To stand out from other colorfully dressed jugglers or acrobats of the day, Wenceslao wore a white tie and tails. This stage attire would become his trademark (contrary to some long-standing accounts, it was not inspired by Edgar Bergen). Wences dreamed of voyaging to the United States in hopes of finding stardom and fortune among the footlights. That almost mythical lure of greasepaint and one-night stands was not lost on Wenceslao Moreno; adopting the simpler stage name "Señor Wences," he packed up one of his dummies and immigrated to the U.S. in 1934.

Wences had hoped for instant stardom in the States, but instead he discovered that the vaudeville scene was virtually extinct when he finally arrived. He was too late; movies and radio were the American public's new favorite pastimes. Ventriloquists had been reduced to accepting lowly gigs at county fairs and seedy nightclubs for survival. Even most of those

venues proved inhospitable to Wences, possibly due in part to his thick Spanish accent. Fortunately he was accepted at the Club Chico in Greenwich Village. For the next two years, Wences struggled for a foothold on foreign soil. Alas, part of the problem was that his act lacked originality: "I was just another ventriloquist with a dummy," he once said of those early years.

But fate sometimes helps to correct such shortcomings. In 1936 while traveling to Chicago by rail, Wences's dummy Pedro was badly damaged in a baggage-car accident. Only the figure's head remained intact. Scheduled to perform that night, Wences was forced to improvise. Backstage, he found a wooden box

Here Johnny reads a wartime movie magazine—
the "Winchell vs. Hitler" headline refers to Walter,
the famed gossip columnist, not Paul.

with a hinged lid and fastened Pedro's severed head inside. By cutting a hole in the rear of the box, he was able to manipulate the dummy's mouth. When the stage manager saw this contraption, he threatened to fire the vent if he included such a grotesque prop in his routine. But Wences had little choice; the head-in-the-box was the only dummy he had.

It almost hurts to envision the moment. When his cue came, Wences stepped into the spotlight with the box under his arm. He told a few jokes to warm up the crowd; maybe he even performed some simple sleight of hand. When the time came to open the box, the vent knew his job was on the line. Just before cracking open the lid he asked the box, in his thick

Spanish accent, "S'awright?" Wences opened the box, suddenly exposing Pedro's disembodied head to the shocked audience.

"S'awright!" said Pedro, before the box loudly snapped shut again.

With Pedro's abrupt appearance and departure, Wences's stage alchemy took hold and the audience burst into uproarious, ecstatic laughter. In less than a minute Wences had created a sure-fire, crowd-pleasing skit that he would use as the centerpiece of his act for the rest of his life. Needless to say, he was not fired after the show.

No matter what the economic or social climate of a given era, in show business a hit is a hit, and somehow that news travels fast. Such was the case with Señor Wences. By 1937, only one year after Pedro's fortuitous accident, word of the hilarious Spanish ventriloquist was swiftly traveling through the U.S. and Europe. Despite the looming threat of a coming world war, the sought-after performer gave command performances to distinguished audiences such as U.S. President Franklin D. Roosevelt and his wife Eleanor, and England's Royal Family.

Between 1936 and 1939 in Britain, Wences appeared on an experimental new "stage," this time an electronic one: television. But war temporarily interrupted his TV career.

In 1940 Wences met Taly Cover, a British-born dancer, backstage at one of his gigs. By this point in his career, the popular performer had thousands of fans. Unfortunately for the love-struck ventriloquist, the captivating

Wences was a master of a ventriloquism technique known as the "distant voice" and could carry on a thoroughly believable two-or-three way conversation on stage. Here, the vent, well into his eighties, and Pedro speak to a third party via telephone.

dancer was not one of them. "The first time he asked me out on a date, I told him I did not like him," she recalls. "But I had to admit, he made me laugh." Eventually the laughter won her over, and the two were married in 1942.

After years of playing on vaudeville-like stages and in supper clubs, Wences, like his other vent and magician contemporaries, found television. Early black-and-white TV proved, for Wences in particular, to be a wonderfully effective new venue in which to present his minimalist approach to comedy. Wences's unusual puppets were smaller than those of vents such as Paul Winchell or Jimmy Nelson, so audiences were not as likely to see the facial

details of his dummies in a live performance. With television, cameras could move in for a close-up of Wences with tiny Johnny or bespectacled Pedro, allowing audiences to get a better look than they ever had before. Wences thrived on TV because the technical capabilities of the camera provided a new intimacy between his viewers and his act, yet viewers still weren't able to catch him moving his lips.

In 1948 Wences made his first American TV appearance on comedian Milton Berle's NBC show, *Texaco Star Theater*. He appeared on Sid Caesar's *Your Show of Shows* with his hen Cecilia. The act must have been a show-stopper, for soon Ed Sullivan wanted Señor Wences on

his program. And Wences was ready; he had his act down pat. The rapid-fire routine he had been developing for nearly thirty years had reached perfection.

It was so good, in fact, that Wences would repeat nearly the same performance on *The Ed Sullivan Show* forty-eight times over the life of the show. For a predictable comedy routine to be so appealing for so long is unusual, but audiences embraced the recurring wackiness of Señor Wences's act, and that wackiness came to define him. The beloved characters that he created were like Charlie Chaplin's Little Tramp or Jackie Gleason's Ralph Kramden—viewers knew exactly what to expect from them. And just the thought of seeing Wences's Johnny or Pedro again made people laugh.

Wences's unique formula for laughs was anything but formulaic; he never relied

Señor Wences meets Donald Duck while on a tour of Walt Disney Studios in the late 1950s. On the right is the vent's tour guide, Walt Disney himself. The specially made puppet of Donald pictured here was used only for publicity appearances.

Taly Moreno, Wences's wife of fifty-nine years, has remained his ardent supporter. After the brouhaha that erupted when Ed Sullivan advised Wences to keep Pedro's box closed during his act, Wences boycotted the show for three years. "What will Wences do without Sullivan?" Taly was asked, to which she replied, "What will Sullivan do without Wences?"

upon the classic setup of a joke followed by a punch line. There were no jokes at all in Wences's skits, only frenetic movement, curious props and odd scraps of conversation. Picture Wences with his tux and serious demeanor, spinning plates, juggling pins, and carrying on a running dialog with his hand or a head-in-the-box—the absurd world he concocted was enough to keep the audience in stitches.

Wences's *Ed Sullivan* routine usually started with Johnny outfitted with googly glass eyes, a blond wig and a tiny doll's body. On some shows he would stuff a handkerchief in the puppet's mouth so that Johnny's usual falsetto would suddenly be muffled. At other times Wences astonished audiences by being able to smoke a cigarette while having Johnny sing at the same time. Sometimes Johnny himself would have a puff and blow smoke rings—a nifty trick, the secret of which Wences never revealed:

45

WENCES:	*Ees goot?*
JOHNNY:	(between puffs) *Ees bery goot!*
WENCES:	*Ees nice?*
JOHNNY:	*Ees bery nice!*

Before the audience finished laughing, Wences, would start in with a physical stunt, like balancing a spinning plate on a stick or juggling. At the same time, he would open the door to Pedro's box:

PEDRO:	*Close de door!*
	(Wences slams it closed, and then quickly reopens it)
WENCES:	*S'awright?*
PEDRO:	*S'awright!*

Wences would immediately slam the box, and the audience would go wild.

Perhaps Wences would then present Cecilia the Hen, a motherly hand puppet who sat nestled in Wences's arms. Cecilia was the very picture of proud motherhood, a puppet whose personality was probably influenced by Wences's own *madré*. While not as eccentric a character as Johnny or Pedro, Cecila still gave audiences plenty of reasons to laugh:

| WENCES: | (Holding an egg) *What is this?* |
| CECILIA: | *My son.* |

Johnny could eat, smoke and drink, all to the amazement of audiences. Wences was not the only vent to use his hand as a puppet; Edgar Bergen and Shari Lewis both performed a similar trick, but neither ever created an enduring character from it. Jimmy Nelson remembers that once when the suitcase carrying his dummies was temporarily lost, he improvised the evening's performance with an imitation of Wences's Johnny.

| WENCES: | *How do you know?* |
| CECILIA: | *I know my bee-zee-niss!* |

The 1950s saw Señor Wences become one of the hardest-working comedy performers in the world. With his makeshift puppets Johnny and Pedro, and other props, the vent continuously fine-tuned his act. One skit included an easel and a pad of paper on which Wences would draw a telephone. He would then attach a handset and start talking into the ridiculous-looking prop, carrying on both sides of an equally ridiculous conversation. He and Pedro would next decide to sing a duet in Spanish, and the unseen Johnny (who'd been hidden behind the easel) would join in, seemingly unable to resist the fun. With Pedro's box furiously opening and shutting, all three would sing—a man in a tux, a head-in-the-box, and an unseen androgynous hand puppet. In another skit, the onstage patter moved so quickly that no conversation was sustained for long—Johnny would practice his do-re-mis, Pedro would refuse to come out, and Wences would move elegantly between the two, talking nonstop all the while. And yet Wences's tone in the midst of all this insanity remained sedate and sophisticated, as if he were a parent amused by his children's antics and unaffected by their oddity. With Wences, the movement onstage was a curious mix of the exaggerated and the restrained.

As bizarre and chaotic as his act might

FLIP CLIP

have seemed to an audience, on stage Señor Wences's act was carefully calculated. He analyzed his sketches with the rigor of a scientist to learn exactly which nuance, inflection, rhythm or gesture best elicited a desired audience reaction. His technical skill as a ventriloquist was flawless. In his book *Other Voices,* the late Stanley Burns, a professional ventriloquist and historian, discusses one of Wences's observations, noting that only five different voices would work in Wences's act. "I have tried it many times," Burns quotes Wences, "and always I find the same thing, in London, in Spain, in Paris, in South America. If I put in two more voices the audience thinks it is some trick I play on them, maybe phonograph records . . . Five gets big applause, but seven, not so big."

Between his Sullivan spots, Wences still played the club circuit, including every casino in Las Vegas. He entertained four U.S. presidents and appeared in shows with Dean Martin and Jerry Lewis, and the great Danny Kaye. "No one worked harder than Wences," Taly said, "but he loved every minute of it. Performing was his life."

During his long career, Wences appeared in thirty-three TV commercials and made countless television guest appearances from 1948 until his retirement in 1986. At times, he created new puppets for these engagements. But since most of these characters appeared only once, and no photographs are known to exist, their names and personalities have been lost in the annals of ventriloquism.

Ed Sullivan's show ended in 1971 and, though Señor Wences would continue to be seen many times on countless reruns of the program for years to come, he—like most ventriloquists—never again had the same presence on TV. There were still occasional appearances on *The Tonight Show Starring Johnny Carson* (Carson, a

Flip Clip

former vent himself, was always a fan of Señor Wences) and other programs, but never enough to sustain the type of celebrity he had enjoyed during Sullivan's heyday. In America, at least, Wences's chosen art form had lost its vital mainstream standing.

So Wences signed up for an extended engagement at the Crazy Horse Saloon in Paris. There he found an establishment that still welcomed variety acts like those from the earlier eras of American vaudeville or European music halls. Señor Wences fit in comfortably with the chorus girls, jugglers, acrobats and magicians for the next seven years of his life. By the end of the show's run in 1978, he was eighty-two years old.

Wences continued to perform through-

out the 1980s, although his age began to affect his performance. Johnny's high-pitched voice was beginning to crack, damaging the lifelike illusion Wences had perfected over decades. The act's lightening-fast timing was slowing down, and Wences started to drop some of his spinning plates. He even broke one of Cecilia's eggs on stage. "My baby! My baby!" she cried.

In 1986 Señor Wences performed with Mickey Rooney and Ann Miller in the road company of Broadway's vaudevillian variety-style musical review *Sugar Babies*. He was ninety years old but got the job, in part because

señor wences at 100 plus

A few years ago, I had a great thrill. It was at the 1996 Academy of Magical Arts awards banquet at the famed Beverly Hilton. The event was big—Hollywood and TV celebrities posed as the paparazzi fired away. That night, a special fellowship award was given to the only performer who was not a magician. It was presented to that multi-gifted ventriloquist whom I'm sure you all know, Señor Wences.

I was lucky to be chosen to present the award to that charming Spanish gentleman who was celebrating his one-hundredth birthday that very evening. He was in great shape for his incredible age. I have a photo of the two of us together and he looks better than I do.

That night, he told me about how, after a

brief stint in the army he entered show business as a juggler, not a vent. While touring South America, the stage manager announced that any performer who required musical accompaniment would not appear on opening night. Wences switched from juggler to ventriloquist on the spot. By that fortuitous decision, we became the recipients of his classic genius.

Wences has performed in every medium from vaudeville, motion pictures and television to nightclubs—including a seven-year engagement at the Crazy Horse Saloon in Paris and an unprecedented forty-eight appearances on *The Ed Sullivan Show*. As I presented the award I showed the audience some of his work on a huge monitor. He was absolutely brilliant.

When Wences used his hand to create Johnny it was sheer magic—he did that trick better than I'd ever seen it done before or since. And the part of his act that always made me howl with laughter was when Pedro would run out of things to say and tell Wences to "close de door" on his box. That was hysterically funny. And Señor Wences's act influenced every vent that came after him.

I had hoped to spend more birthdays with him, as I did two years later when he turned 102. Unfortunately, he left us just days after reaching 103. No one can live forever, but Wences thrilled us with his remarkable skill for so many years that his memory will live forever.

—PAUL WINCHELL

Wences in the 1970s, still performing; still "S'awright!"

Taly had told the producers he was seventy-five. After six weeks, Señor Wences decided to retire. He was, indeed, tired.

Wences spent most of his last thirteen years in New York City, where he lived with Taly in the apartment they had shared for decades, just a block from the old Ed Sullivan Theater. It was a proximity that once had allowed him to easily accept any last-minute bookings on Sullivan's show, but those days were gone. Occasionally, the aging Señor would visit family in Spain or make special appearances on telethons or local talk shows, usually bringing Pedro for a quick, crowd-pleasing "S'awright!" In 1996, New York's Friar's Club honored him on his one-hundredth birthday with a huge party, in which the guest list included old show biz friends and a few fellow ventriloquists, most notably Paul Winchell. "People wondered why he would only talk to me," the bilingual Winchell recalled. "I told them, 'it's because I'm the only one who can speak Spanish with him!'"

Mostly, Wences enjoyed taking walks with Taly and visiting with friends. As magician and friend Norm Nielsen remembers of the time, "Whenever I would visit Señor Wences and his wife in New York City, we would walk to their favorite restaurant. He

carried a cane, but was very spry even at his age. He would begin his meal with a Harvey's Bristol Cream, then a hot soup (he loved soup) and a full meal and dessert. Then he would take his cloth napkin and fold and twist it until it looked like a duck and it would drink out of his glass." Fellow diners would be stunned and delighted, proof that age never diminished Wences's desire for and love of performing. And although Wenceslao Moreno died on April 20, 1999, just three days after his 103rd birthday, Señor Wences the comic entity endures.

Of all the ventriloquists from the art form's Golden Age on TV, none occupy the unique place in the public consciousness that Señor Wences does. New York City has even honored his memory by designating a block of West 54th Street alongside the Ed Sullivan Theater as Señor Wences Way. The fact that a Spanish ventriloquist could win the hearts of America with his talking fist and boxed dummy head says it all. Those too young to have enjoyed Wences's magic firsthand might have heard or used the phrase "S'awright!" without being aware of the man who coined it. And how many people, inspired by Wences, have drawn a talking face on their closed fist to entertain a child? It still works like a charm. All thanks to the good Señor.

Wences adopted his dapper look when he was still living in Spain, long before Charlie McCarthy donned his top hat and tails.

49

NAME: PEDRO

ARRIVED ON THE SCENE: 1936

DISTINGUISHING CHARACTERISTICS: handlebar mustache, large specs, lack of body, general surliness

Wences's world famous head-in-the-box with the gravel voice, whose quick mood changes might nowadays merit a visit to the doctor, was born as a result of a nasty wooden dummy decapitation in 1936. Though he could be grumpy, mumbling "Pedro not available" or "Close de door," Wences always treated this disembodied head with utmost respect and honored Pedro's wishes when the head chose not to perform. Pedro's appeal led other celebrities, such as Milton Berle, to try out variations in the routine and appear in the box themselves.

FAMED REMARK: "S'awright!"

NAME: JOHNNY

ARRIVED ON THE SCENE: "discovered" some time around 1900 to 1915, while Wences was still a schoolboy, after the young vent spilled ink on his hand

DISTINGUISHING CHARACTERISTICS: bed-head, googly eyes, removable body

Johnny was Wences's lifelong stage partner—a dummy that the vent really did carry everywhere. Wences and his sweet hand puppet shared an appreciation for beautiful Spanish songs, cigarettes and *The Ed Sullivan Show*. Johnny is also featured along with Wences in the 1947 musical *Mother Wore Tights*.

FAMED REMARK: "Dee-fee-cult for you. Easy for me!"

NAME: CECILIA

ARRIVED ON THE SCENE: 1948

DISTINGUISHING CHARACTERISTICS:

knit shawl, extreme neurosis, bejeweled spectacles (occasionally)

Wences created the anxious hen for his appearance on Sid Caesar's program *Your Show of Shows* in 1948. His hilarious act then caught the eye of Ed Sullivan, and the rest, as Wences might say, was "hiz-tree."

FAMED REMARK: "I know my bee-zee-niss!"

NAME: O-NO

ARRIVED ON THE SCENE: in a commercial with Wences in 1948

DISTINGUISHING CHARACTERISTICS:

bug eyes, crazy hair, being related to Johnny

Little is known about this clown character, a more elaborate hand puppet in the style of Johnny. Also like Johnny, O-No appeared androgynous. He or she made only a few brief appearances on *The Ed Sullivan Show* in the 1950s and in some of Wences's many TV commercials between 1948 and 1970.

NAME: ATILANO

ARRIVED ON THE SCENE: unknown

DISTINGUISHING CHARACTERISTICS:

a wooden dummy in a Señor Wences routine—very odd indeed!

Some reports identify this tiny boy dummy as Wences's first slotted-mouth ventriloquist figure. Atilano made few appearances during Wences's TV years, probably because the vent already had his hands full dealing with Johnny, Pedro and Cecilia—often all three at the same time.

Flip Clip

ed sullivan: the ventriloquist's best friend

Why did ventriloquism go out of style? Paul Winchell retorts: *"The Ed Sullivan Show* got cancelled, that's why."

Winchell's observation is on the money: ventriloquism never had a more enthusiastic media cheerleader than the eminent Ed Sullivan. On his now-historic television variety show, which ran for twenty-two seasons from 1948 until 1971, Ed Sullivan regularly included ventriloquists on the eclectic vaudeville-style show bill. In fact, *The Ed Sullivan Show* became a celebrated launching pad for vents.

Sullivan, who personally booked all of the acts that appeared on his hour-long program, had an unmatched eye for picking talent and was determined there would be at least one featured act that appealed to every viewer's taste, despite the wide-ranging demographics of his huge television audience. If Mom didn't like the Borscht Belt comic who caused Dad to bust a gut, she only need wait a few minutes for the romantic Irish tenor to soothe her. Big Sis could scream along with the studio audience for the latest teen idol, while the kiddies giggled with delight at a dog act, acrobat or ventriloquist.

As a variety show host, Sullivan was the medium's most unlikely success story. His characteristic—and much parodied—hunched-over Richard Nixon posture and Boris Karloff-in-makeup face, coupled with his famously

wooden turns of phrase—"Tonight, we have a rilly big shoo for you"—broke all of TV-land's conventions. However, Sullivan's lack of onstage grace endeared him to his viewers, who warmed to his Everyman personality and to his unassuming response to being one of television's biggest names. Audiences trusted Ed Sullivan to entertain them, to fill their dens and living rooms with talent, laughs, tears and applause every Sunday night at eight o'clock. And he dutifully fulfilled those expectations for more than two decades.

In the 1930s and 1940s, before his days on television, Ed Sullivan had been a veritable media Jack-of-all-trades. After years as a New York newspaperman—first a sportswriter and then a noted gossip columnist—Sullivan turned to radio in the 1940s, and CBS asked him to host a television show in 1948. By the modern standards of slick, handsome, high-energy TV personalities, CBS's choice to hire the dour Sullivan as host is mystifying. But the unlikely pairing of Sullivan and a newly conceived variety show called *The Toast of the Town* played a key role in the history of television and ventriloquism.

Memorable moments abounded throughout the run of the show. Despite negative critical reviews, it was a hit from the start. Sullivan was able to book top talent to headline each show, from Dean Martin and Jerry Lewis to

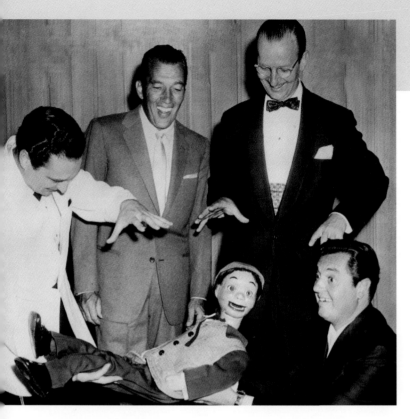

Magician Aldo Richiardi, Ed Sullivan, and magician/ventriloquist Jay Marshall attempt to levitate Velvel, as vent Rickie Layne kneels and throws his voice, in the mid 1950s.

Fred Astaire to Julie Andrews. He even hosted an occasional heavyweight boxing match. By 1956 *The Toast of the Town* had been renamed *The Ed Sullivan Show*—which is what everyone had always called it anyway. During that same year, on one historic Sunday night, Sullivan's ratings broke all existing records when Elvis "The Pelvis" Presley appeared in the most famous of all his television performances.

What marked this particular Elvis appearance was Sullivan's puritanical decision not to shoot the gyrating singer from the waist down. Sullivan's choice left TV viewers titillated by the studio audience's crazed screams, allowing them to imagine an even more suggestive and sexier Elvis than reality held. This segment is arguably one of the most memorable in TV history, and like so many other historic TV

events, it happened on Sullivan's show. Other rock 'n' roll icons to grace the Sullivan stage included the Rolling Stones (who did such a suggestive rendition of "Satisfaction" that they found themselves briefly banned from the show), Janis Joplin, Peter, Paul and Mary, and The Doors (also banned after their performance, but unlike the Stones, for good). And of course, the Fab Four, who made their U.S. television debut on *The Ed Sullivan Show* and subsequently launched Beatlemania across the land.

But rock bands were only one part of Sullivan's mix. Right alongside them were pop stars, renowned actors and Broadway performers, as well as stand-up comics, jugglers, acrobats, accordion players, plate-spinners, puppets, and, of course, ventriloquists. Each of the scheduled performers possessed varying degrees of sophistication, but it is well known that Ed Sullivan loved his ventriloquists the best. Sullivan was noted for giving unknown vents a chance and, by his very support, turning them into stars.

Paul Winchell and Jimmy Nelson both credit *The Ed Sullivan Show* with jump-starting their careers. Winchell made the first of his six appearances on Sullivan in 1948, and he will always hold the significant honor of being the

show's first featured vent act. When twenty-two-year-old Nelson made his network TV debut in 1950, Sullivan mistakenly cut the poor kid's act short, making up for it by inviting the lad back a few weeks later. Nelson would go on to tread the Sullivan boards six more times during the 1950s.

Edgar Bergen, a true vaudevillian from the old days, appeared five times on Sullivan's show, as did preeminent sock puppeteer Shari Lewis. Señor Wences, one of Sullivan's favorite belly talkers, lived conveniently around the block from the Sullivan theater. He appeared forty-eight times, since he lived so close to the theater that Sullivan could call upon him at the last minute to pinch-hit for a no-show act. Wences's unique, quirky place in entertainment history was solidified because of his Sullivan connection. Indeed, no retrospective of *The Ed Sullivan Show* is complete without the footage of Señor Wences and his unforgettable puppet cast.

Sullivan turned to other vents as well. He featured Bob Evans with his fast-talking dummy Jerry O'Leary, Willie Tyler and his Afro-coiffed buddy Lester (who would go on to achieve great popularity on rival network NBC's *Rowan and Martin's Laugh-In*) and Rickie Layne, with his wooden-headed Borscht Belt brat Velvel. Sullivan's roster includes vaguely familiar names such as Dennis Spicer, Chris

Paul Winchell became the first of many ventriloquists who appeared on Ed Sullivan's variety show.

Kirby, Dick Weston, Clifford Quest, Russo Louis, Cris Cross and Arthur Worsley. Admittedly, most of these performers have by now drifted into obscurity. But that doesn't diminish their place in Ed Sullivan's historic little black book of talent. These vents form an elite and noble club, that could be aptly dubbed The Honorable Society of Sullivan Vents. And alongside them, Sullivan also featured other puppet acts, such as Jim Henson and his Muppets, long before their *Sesame Street* and *Muppet Show* days, and a cloyingly cute, rubber Italian mouse named Topo Gigio, who became a staple of the show.

During the unprecedented run of *The Ed Sullivan Show*, CBS managed to practically monopolize the ratings for the Sunday night slot. By 1971, however, after having presented more than ten thousand acts to millions of TV viewers over the course of those twenty-two seasons in twenty-three years, Sullivan's long reign came to a close. At the time, the Vietnam war divided America, and cultural values and tastes were shifting. With his show's cancellation went the last opportunity for American audiences to see the type of vaudevillian spectacle that for more than a century had been such a vital part of the country's entertainment history. While the decade that followed offered other popular variety shows such as *The Carol Burnett Show* and *Sonny and Cher*, none came close to Sullivan's entertainment smorgasbord, or his universal appeal. He and his show were one of a kind.

Ed Sullivan died of esophageal cancer at age seventy-two on October 13, 1974. No doubt on that day the dummies cried, as vents around the world mourned the loss of a very good friend. Indeed, Sullivan continues to be dearly missed, as evidenced by the 1992 special *The Very Best of The Ed Sullivan Show*, Volume 2. At the close of the documentary, a ninety-five-year-old Señor Wences, wearing his classic bow tie and tux and very large glasses, performs with Pedro:

WENCES: *Sul-ee-van?*

PEDRO: *Sul-ee-van. Yeah.*
Goot friend.

WENCES: *Goot friend, eh?*

PEDRO: *Goot friend.*

WENCES: *Nice special?*

PEDRO: *The best.*

WENCES: *The best. He bery intelligent, bery dynamic, bery serious.*

PEDRO: *Bery serious.*

WENCES: *(indecipherable compliment to Pedro)*

PEDRO: *Thank you.*

WENCES: *You're welcome. Give me a kiss. Thank you.*

PEDRO: *You're welcome.*

The box closed. But the Sullivan impact on the vent world continues on video.

WINCHELL: *Good evening, ladies and gentlemen,*
I'm Paul Winchell here with
my little wooden friend Jerry Mahoney.

JERRY: *Yeah, he always explains that*
so you won't think he's the dummy!

FLIP-CLIP

paul winchell

Flip Clip

An utterly confused Paul Winchell sat on the stage during a rehearsal of *The Ed Sullivan Show,* his dummy Jerry Mahoney on his knee. Winchell's agent had finagled a coveted spot on the show for the twenty-six-year-old ventriloquist. But here at his first important rehearsal, just when the act seemed to be going well, Sullivan signaled for him to stop. This was to be Paul Winchell's big break, and from the look of things, it wasn't going to happen.

"Sullivan said he could hear me just fine, but not Jerry," Winchell recalls. So the ventriloquist tried again, this time speaking his lines very softly. When he came to Jerry's lines, the vent compensated with an extra loud delivery. It worked a little better, but in the director's booth, Sullivan was still shaking his head. Winchell, although worried, kept trying. Seeing that Sullivan was growing impatient, Winchell lost all hope for a spot on the show.

He was baffled. "I thought maybe I was discovering that by some odd technical fluke ventriloquism wouldn't work on TV."

Just before Sullivan asked him to leave the stage, the performer glanced upward and noticed that whenever Jerry spoke, the soundman would move the microphone above the dummy's head. The technician had never worked with a ventriloquist and, like every audience, he thought Winchell was "throwing his voice," so he put the mike above the

dummy. Winchell paused his act and instructed the technician to keep the microphone over his head and, "I told him, no matter what, don't move it."

Of course, it worked. Paul Winchell and Jerry Mahoney performed that night, and for the first time, a ventriloquist was featured on *The Ed Sullivan Show.* It would be the most significant first in TV history as far as vents were concerned, and Sullivan would prove to be every vent's best friend (see page 52). The comic duo would perform on Sullivan's show five more times over the course of its Sunday night reign, helping to launch a national television program

FLIP CLIP

for the ventriloquist that would one day rank near *The Howdy Doody Show* in popularity.

What Edgar Bergen and Charlie McCarthy were to radio, Paul Winchell and Jerry Mahoney were to television: they shaped the early medium and practically invented the idea of children's programming. As a ventriloquist, Winchell pioneered technical effects that are still used today (how ironic that his TV debut was almost undone by a technical difficulty). All the while, Winchell and his mischievous, red-haired friend Mahoney made ventriloquism

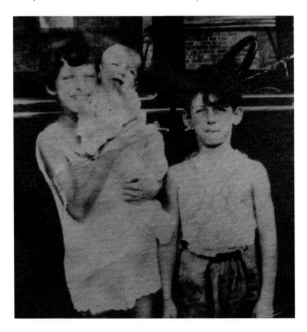

Paul Winchell, in the late 1920s. The young vent is around age six and poses with his sisters Ruth (left) and baby Rita.

fun, entertaining and inspiring viewers young and old for more than fifteen years:

WINCHELL: *Jerry, why don't you behave
                     yourself?*

JERRY: *Well, I could be good . . .
                     for a quarter.*

WINCHELL: *Oh, why can't you be more
                     like me?*

JERRY: *And be good for nuttin'?!*

Winchell—or Winch, as Jerry affectionately referred to him—was bound for show biz from the beginning. Born in Manhattan on December 21, 1922, his family relocated shortly thereafter to Brooklyn's Coney Island. "You could almost say I was born and raised on the midway," Winchell says as he recalls his youth. "I spent my childhood years going to the sideshows—'The Alligator-Skinned Man,' 'The Rubber-Faced Man'. . . all that sort of stuff. It was all amazing to me."

Couple his Coney Island roots with his fascination with Edgar Bergen, and it makes sense that Winchell ended up on stage. It was Bergen's first feature film, *The Goldwyn Follies* (1938), that confirmed the young boy's ambition. Though young Winchell had always been a fan of Bergen's radio programs, he says he was shocked to discover while sitting in the movie theater that the popular performer was a

Winchell made such a splash in his 1936 debut appearance on CBS radio's *Major Bowes' Original Amateur Hour* that he soon joined the host's national touring company. Major Bowes (right) stands proudly by his new discovery, the fourteen-year-old vent and his first dummy, Terry Mahoney.

ventriloquist. He, like so many of Bergen's radio fans, had simply assumed that Charlie McCarthy was a flesh-and-blood sidekick. "I saw this little piece of wood sit up and come to life and something struck me. I said to myself right there in the dark, 'I gotta learn how to do that.'"

The excited youngster purchased a small instructional booklet written by Bergen that he saw advertised in a magazine:

BE THE LIFE OF THE PARTY!
THROW YOUR VOICE!
LEARN VENTRILOQUISM!
Send 10 Cents for Booklet

The book came with a special apparatus—a "ventro-whistle"—to be placed secretly inside the mouth. Winchell found the device unsatisfactory as it only allowed him to create high-pitched bird calls. Bergen's book proved more useful. It stressed the basics: Standing before a mirror and saying the alphabet without moving the lips, particularly the difficult letters B, F, M, P, V, W and Y, which required replacement sounds, like S for F or T for P. There were also diagrams showing proper tongue positions vital to any ventriloquist's technique. This new information proved a revelation to Winchell, and in a short time he was throwing his voice. Winchell proved to have a natural affinity for ventriloquism, a trait some respected proprietors of the art believe is

The earliest known photograph of Winchell and Jerry Mahoney, circa 1938. The wooden dummy pictured here was carved by Frank Marshall and resides in the permanent collection of the Smithsonian Institution.

inborn, likening the skill to being ambidextrous or double jointed. As the boy grew, he developed another talent: commercial art. Paul and his parents determined he would have more income potential from drawing magazine and newspaper ads than by making a dummy talk.

In 1936, while attending Manhattan's High School for Industrial Arts, Winchell's art teacher agreed to give him class credit for making a ventriloquist's puppet. As a tribute to this instructor, Jero Magon, Winchell named

FLIP CLIP

the early dummy Terry Mahoney (later this homage was reinforced when Winchell changed the dummy's first name to Jerry). Magon quickly recognized the boy's talent when he saw the young vent present a dead-on impression of Edgar Bergen at a school function. "Like many things in my life, it was all very serendipitous," Winchell recalls, "Mr. Magon suggested that I do a demonstration for the school's principal, who just happened to have a friend who did a radio show for amateur talents." The principal's friend was Major Bowes of the popular radio show *Major Bowes' Original Amateur Hour*. Though the fourteen-year-old "was only doing it for fun," his appearance on the radio show ignited a chain of events that affected his life for good. All very serendipitous, indeed.

The show's premise was simple: Each week amateur entertainers competed for a coveted one hundred-dollar prize, an award based on the number of votes tallied from listener phone-ins. Several performers who had first appeared on *Major Bowes' Original Amateur Hour* went on to achieve stardom, such as operatic tenor Robert Merrill, singer/dancer Vera Ellen and, most notably, Frank Sinatra. When Winchell took his turn at Bowes's microphone, his Bergen impersonation proved to be a turning point. The young vent and Terry, his art class dummy, broke the record for audience votes. What follows is an excerpt from that first delightful performance, which was preserved on audio tape:

TERRY: *Oh, do I get to meet Major Bowes?*

WINCHELL: *Oh no, Terry, you'll get too excited.*

TERRY: *Why, I've never been excited in my life . . . except once.*

WINCHELL: *Oh, and when was that?*

TERRY: *Well, there I was, headed straight for a truck parked in the middle of the road.*

Winchell: *Oh my.*

TERRY: *I jammed on the brakes, but it was useless.*

WINCHELL: *Gosh Terry, you were in a dilemma.*

TERRY: *No, it was a DeSoto!*

At the time, Winchell thought his Bowes appearance was a fluke. Just two weeks later, however, Winchell received a call from Major Bowes, who offered him a part in one of the *Amateur Hour*'s traveling units touring throughout the United States. The job paid thirty-five dollars a week. "This was a time when my father was supporting a whole household on only twelve bucks a week . . . I fell over backwards."

After considering Bowes's offer, Paul decided to "give it a try for a little while, which turned into a year, which turned into a year and a half." Almost overnight, the fifteen-year-old found himself performing in theaters across

This handsome 1948 publicity photo was taken just as Paul Winchell stood on the threshold of fame. It is also the best remaining photograph of Frank Marshall's original version of Jerry Mahoney.

the country, while, ". . . back home in New York, the truant officer is looking for me."

In 1937 the Bowes troupe landed in Hollywood, a mythic place in young Paul Winchell's view that offered golden—and fleeting—career opportunities. "I'm a kid from Brooklyn and I think to myself, 'If I leave town with Major Bowes's show, that will be it. I'll never have a chance like this again.' " So he took his dummy, abandoned the next show and decided to stay in town.

"I was in Hollywood and I was gonna be a big star . . . and I had a rude awakening," as Winchell describes what happened during his first year in the entertainment capital. Though his intention was to take filmland by storm, he instead found himself living on Los Angeles's Main Street, by then a seedy holdover from the Great Depression, a.k.a. Skid Row. The teenager had ten dollars in his pocket, and the cost of his daily dinner was ten cents. It wasn't long before the math left Winchell hungry. Desperate for work, the kid knocked on the door of the Paris Inn, a third-rate nightclub he spotted from the street. What transpired next stands as testament to Winchell's innate ingenuity, sense of self-preservation and natural-born showmanship—qualities that would serve him well throughout his life.

Winchell approached the club's manager about his act. To the boss's "How much?" the boy promised that his services were free of charge, adding that if he was no good the proprietor could order him off the stage "What's

By the time this photo was taken in the late 1940s, Winchell was touring with top-name big bands and starting to make his first TV appearances.

the catch?" the manager asked, still unconvinced. Winchell's only request was that if his act got applause from the audience, the owner would toss a coin onto the stage.

Assessing that he had nothing to lose, the manager allowed the boy to perform that very night. The Paris Inn was, by Winchell's account, as run-down as a downtown bar got in 1937, its audience consisting mostly of barflies who were decidedly not there to see a fifteen-year-old ventriloquist and his dummy. "To call it a tough crowd would be an understatement," Winchell reminisces. Good fortune found him that night, as Jerry leveled his first bratty insult ("Aw, yer mudder peddles papers!") and from somewhere in the smoke-filled darkness came genuine laughs. "I couldn't believe it. The people applauded and the boss threw out a coin. So Jerry started to make jokes about it. He said,

FLIP CLIP

'Oh, Winch, we're gonna eat tonight!' " The rapt audience took the bait and began throwing more loose change onto the stage, until "I made a tidy little sum. And the boss said, 'You can work here for free every night.' "

Winchell played the Paris Inn for several weeks and began to make a decent living. Or as he puts it, "I started thinking I was a real Big Shot." Luckily, during his Paris Inn stint Winchell landed a theatrical agent and began to work other more respectable nightclub venues, "where they had a full orchestra and served dinner. Men wore suits and ladies wore hats." The best of these gigs was in Denver, where Winchell met bandleader Ted Weems, who was popular nationally in the 1930s and 1940s. Weems asked the young ventriloquist to join his tour at $175 per week. "I swallowed my tongue, my tie—everything—to try to keep a straight face," Winchell recollects. "I was still just sixteen years old. My pop was still back in New York making twelve bucks a week. That's when I became a real pro."

Winchell's transition to professional ventriloquist also dictated his graduation from amateur dummy. While appearing in Chicago with Weems's band, he looked up local puppet maker Frank Marshall (page 100). "He was very fast and made the dummy in a week. Only problem was that it looked just like me." Fearing that audiences wouldn't buy into the illusion of a Paul Winchell clone, the ventriloquist opted for another dummy in Marshall's shop which he liked better. This red-haired dummy became the original version of Jerry and Winchell performed with it until the early 1950s. Currently, this figure resides in the permanent collection of the Smithsonian Institution.

Paul Winchell has always admitted that the Jerry Mahoney character began as a good-

In this 1950s publicity photo, Winchell appears as dapper as his idol Edgar Bergen, who also fancied the tux for portraits.

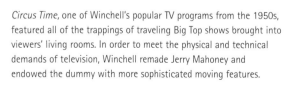

Circus Time, one of Winchell's popular TV programs from the 1950s, featured all of the trappings of traveling Big Top shows brought into viewers' living rooms. In order to meet the physical and technical demands of television, Winchell remade Jerry Mahoney and endowed the dummy with more sophisticated moving features.

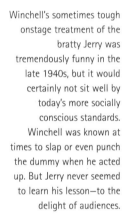

Winchell's sometimes tough onstage treatment of the bratty Jerry was tremendously funny in the late 1940s, but it would certainly not sit well by today's more socially conscious standards. Winchell was known at times to slap or even punch the dummy when he acted up. But Jerry never seemed to learn his lesson—to the delight of audiences.

encountered daily. Always generously spouting Bowery Boy-like regional dialect such as "dis" and "dat," the ventriloquist made it easy for fans to en-vision Jerry playing stickball or running through the spray of an open fire hydrant amid New York's inner-city asphalt neighborhoods.

Like many comics and ventrilo-quists of the early 1940s, most of Winchell's professional work came from tour-ing the country's sup-

humored imitation of his idol Edgar Bergen's dummy, Charlie McCarthy. When it became obvious that his accidental vocation was a permanent profession, he gave Jerry his own unique identity. While McCarthy, with his *Esquire* magazine-inspired monocle and tux, was mischievous and brash, Mahoney grew to resemble a rambunctious street urchin, cleaned up, dressed and combed for church—a loaded pea-shooter cunningly concealed in his hip pocket. Streetwise and tough, the Mahoney persona mirrored the same savvy kid Brooklyn-raised Winchell had been—or at least like those ruffians young Paul must have

per clubs. In Winchell's case, these gigs were often in conjunction with many of the popular big bands of the day, led by such legends as Woody Herman, Benny Goodman and Tommy Dorsey. He developed entire routines during which he and Jerry would trade comic banter with the band's leader. Each show was a variety review of sorts, featuring solo singers, drummers or dancers and, between musical sets, other acts such as magicians or jugglers. Winchell and Mahoney provided the comic thread that held it all together. "I'd work with, say, Chico Marx and his orchestra," Winchell says, "and we'd do a whole bit."

FLIP–CLIP

WINCHELL: *Oh, Chico, I haven't introduced you to Jerry have I?*

CHICO: (In his customary exaggerated Italian accent): *No, I've-a not meet-a the kid.*

WINCHELL: *Jerry, meet Chico.*

JERRY: *Howd'ya do?* (Bows head)

CHICO: *Howd'ya do?* (Bows head)

JERRY: *Howd'ya do?* (Bows head)

CHICO: *Howd'ya do?* (Bows head)

JERRY: (Looking at Winchell): *Who's workin' his head?*

Show business trade paper reviews were enthusiastic about Winchell throughout the 1940s as he played club after club, still performing with the country's top big bands. Such positive responses led to young Winchell's first encounter with television, the medium that would make him a star. The ventriloquist's first television appearance was in late 1946 on a variety-style program produced live from a New York City department store. Since few Americans actually had television sets, most viewers came to the store to watch. For Winchell, it all took some getting used to: "The lights were so hot that my sleeves had to be rolled up. I got a burn on my forearm from my belt buckle." But despite Winchell's problems, TV was catching on fast. "I remember driving through Manhattan, looking up at rooftops and seeing those metal antennas growing and multiplying like trees in a forest. I realized then that TV was gonna be big." And Winchell was in on the ground floor.

After his nearly-derailed debut on *The Ed Sullivan Show*, he was invited to star—sort of—in his own show, sharing the bill with a popular mind reader known as The Great Dunninger. The curious format for *The Bigelow Show* (named for the rug and carpet manufacturer that sponsored it) split the program into two fifteen-minute segments: one featuring Dunninger's psychic feats, the other spotlighting the comic duo of Winchell and Mahoney. "The show was so disjointed that it was as if Dunninger and I didn't even know each other. We each did our fifteen minutes, then we would say good night and we didn't even talk to each other. No integration; no bits together."

The Bigelow Show was a short-lived experiment and was soon cancelled. However, the experience provided Winchell and his dummy with enough positive exposure to soon take on the job of host—or hosts—on the Speidel Watchband Co.'s, *What's My Name?* Premiering in 1951, *What's My Name?* was one of a genre of programs known in the entertainment business as a "salmagundi" (like the famed stew, a mixture of miscellany) comprised of unrelated acts. Equal parts variety and quiz show, each episode featured Winchell in comedic or dramatic sketches and musical numbers—all of which contained hidden clues related to the identity of the evening's designated famous person. At the end of the show, contestants were asked to guess the

As early as 1951, when Winchell and Mahoney began hosting the Speidel Watchband Co's *What's My Name?* On NBC-TV, Jerry had many costume choices for his various skits. By the looks of things here, Winchell didn't always agree with the dummy's sartorial taste.

65

Flip Clip

name. Often Jerry Mahoney starred in the skits with Winchell, although on occasion the vent would perform solo, as an actor, dancer or singer. Because the program showcased Winchell's versatile talents as a comedian, dancer, crooner and ventriloquist, executives at NBC took notice and in 1953 offered him his own show.

The Paul Winchell-Jerry Mahoney Show began airing weeknights at eight o'clock as basically a non-quiz show version of What's My Name? The show was primarily oriented for adults rather than children—a choice that reflected the prevailing attitude toward ventriloquism at the time. It featured guest stars as diverse and esteemed as Angela Lansbury, Sir Cedric Hardwicke and Peter Lorre. Each episode included comic skits with Winchell and Jerry, musical and dance interludes, and dramatic sketches featuring elaborate sets and costumes. The opportunity and challenge of having his own show encouraged Winchell to create new material and try unexplored methods of manipulating his puppets. He realized that attracting a TV audience—and keeping it tuned in—was

it's good to have heroes

When I was growing up, the majority of my friends chose their heroes from the world of sports. I was decidedly different. My hero was Paul Winchell.

From the first moment Paul Winchell and Jerry Mahoney flickered across my television screen, I became enthralled. I watched in wonder as Jerry joked, sang, played the drums and even danced. In a child's eyes it was a fairy tale come to life. The wooden boy had become real, and I sensed in my heart that I was witnessing pure magic.

From that moment on, my life changed. While my contemporaries attended Little League practice, I'd be at home rehearsing with my very own Jerry Mahoney puppet. As my friends honed their batting and outfielding skills, I labored to drink a glass of water while singing "Fine and Dandy" (a nearly impossible feat, I was relieved to eventually learn—but not before almost choking).

My parents would frequently assume I had friends in my room because of the various voices they heard emanating from behind the closed door. Too often they were wrong. It was just Jerry and me. My mother and father were reasonable people and discussions about psychiatric treatment eventually ended.

Ultimately I discovered that thousands of Jerry Mahoney figures had been sold across the country. Paul Winchell had inspired a devoted following. I was not alone.

Winchell would eventually become known as "The Television Ventriloquist." He and his steadfast companions Jerry Mahoney and Knucklehead Smiff would dominate TV screens for more than three decades—quite an impressive run compared to today's standards. Winchell's continual presence on TV would eventually garner him millions of fans across the world and prove a significant influence within the world of ventriloquism.

Beyond the vent world, Winchell sought new directions in which to utilize his genius. Besides becoming an accomplished painter and sculptor, he invented the first working prototype of an artificial human heart, and he also holds an impressive number of patents in a variety of technical fields. Paul Winchell is unmistakably that rare breed of individual who would have excelled in any field he chose to pursue.

All of us who have been touched by his performances must consider ourselves fortunate that he became an entertainer in our own time. His made his mark in an era of show business that seemed much kinder, gentler and certainly more innocent.

Not often does a guy get to meet his heroes. I consider myself privileged. Over the years "Winch" has become a close personal friend. His body of work continues to impress me as I now appreciate his virtuosity from the level of a fellow professional. Inspiration is often found in the unlikeliest of places. Had there not been a Winchell, there might not have been an Alf.

Like I said, it's good to have heroes.

—PAUL FUSCO
Creator and puppeteer of TV's Alf

66

essential to the success of his program. To stand out in the competitive variety-show scene, he reflects now that he intuitively knew that he had to "get the dummy off my lap."

The Paul Winchell-Jerry Mahoney Show served as a forum for some of Winchell's most inspired and innovative ideas—ideas that would revolutionize the art of ventriloquism and puppetry forever. Because Winchell realized that physical dexterity added another dimension to his dummy's personality, he personally carved at least three duplicate versions of Jerry and endowed the new figures with special talents. Winchell's new dummies could levitate, fly, swim, hang upside-down, swing from trees, ride bikes, horses or sleds, drive cars, box, strum a ukulele or play the violin. Whatever a given skit called for, the vent imaginatively adapted his puppets for the purpose.

The best example of Winchell's ingenuity was how Jerry Mahoney came to possess his uncannily human-like hands. Not long after his first appearance on television, Winchell performed at Atlanta's Lawson General Hospital—an institution devoted to aiding amputees. During his act the ventriloquist noticed two men in the audience, seated next to each other. One had lost his right arm, the other his left. Together they worked as a team, operating as one person. Using each other's hand, they would

clap and, through a well-practiced bit of synchronization, they'd roll, light and smoke cigarettes. Winchell—who was always fascinated with medical technology (see "From Mr. Winkle to Dr. Winchell," page 72)—saw a demonstration of various advanced prosthetics on his tour of the hospital. A pair of realistic artificial hands impressed him and gave him an important idea: puppeteers could combine choreography with prosthetics to give a character a more convincing illusion of life. Television was the perfect place to test this new concept.

Winchell fashioned specially designed sleeves for Jerry, into which a separate puppeteer would then insert his arms and hold small artificial hands. Hidden by a curtain behind the dummy, the puppeteer synchronized his movements with Winchell, who manipulated Jerry's head and mouth as usual. It took hours of practice, but the resulting effect paid off: Jerry was able to pick up items, gesture, and physically interact with Winchell and other actors on the show. Before long, the prosthetics proved awkward, pressing Winchell to devise a

The earliest incarnation of *The Paul Winchell-Jerry Mahoney Show* in 1953 was geared mostly for grown-ups and featured as guest stars many respected stage and screen actors, including, as pictured here, Angela Lansbury.

This behind-the-scenes photo, taken in the 1970s on the set of Winchell's Saturday morning show *The Little News,* illustrates how the vent worked with a puppeteer partner—or hand actor—to create moving fingers for his dummies. The puppeteers are wearing special blue clothing and hoods, which made them invisible to TV viewers.

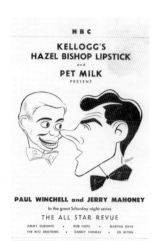

It's clear in this 1952 trade ad that Winchell's stardom equalled that of many performers who are now regarded as show business legends. Perhaps if more visual records of his work on television from the 1950s survived, Winchell too would be a household name.

specially sized, skin-colored glove, which enabled the puppeteer to use his own hands. This innovation worked to even greater effect, and Winchell exploited it in all ways imaginable. When a sketch called for Jerry to juggle, a master juggler was hired to be Jerry's hands, likewise with magicians or trumpeters—whatever talent fit the bill, a professional was called in to act as Jerry's limbs. One memorable trick placed Jerry behind a full set of drums, where he broke into an energetic solo worthy of the great jazz drummer Buddy Rich, which was actually performed by an unknown "stunt drummer" hidden behind a curtain. Another skit teamed Winchell and Mahoney in a lively tap dance, the dummy's oversized pant legs effectively hiding the human arms inside them. These innovative illusions made Jerry Mahoney seem remarkably real, and quickly became standard on all of Winchell's shows.

These playful gimmicks and the physical manipulations that created them set the standard for other ventriloquists and puppeteers for many years to come. Most notably, Jim Henson, creator of the Muppet empire, utilized techniques pioneered by Winchell and was highly influenced by his work. But Henson didn't do his technical magic until the late 1950s. In terms of implementing these innovative physical elements into a ventriloquial performance, Winchell was the very first, and certainly one of a kind. Vent historians marvel at tapes of Winchell dating as far back as 1953, when he would perform wonderfully choreographed and flawless

sketches with his souped-up dummies. On at least one occasion, Jerry Mahoney performed a Christmas brass bell duet with Winchell, while simultaneously the two sang a song.

By 1954 network ratings surveys made it clear that, while many adults certainly enjoyed his show, Paul Winchell's most ardent fans were children. After all, Jerry was constantly getting into the type of trouble any grade school kid could relate to, whether it was bringing home a note from the teacher or keeping a messy bedroom. So the show was renamed *Winchell-Mahoney Time* and NBC switched its time slot to its Saturday morning lineup. Broadcast nationally from New York City, *Winchell-Mahoney Time* had a studio audience of energetic kids and a stage designed to invoke a backyard clubhouse setting. Soon, Jerry Mahoney became every kid's sharp-witted best buddy:

WINCHELL: *Now Jerry, let's pretend I'm the dentist and you're my patient. Open your mouth.*

JERRY: *Aaaahhh.*

WINCHELL: *Wider, please.*

JERRY: *Aaaaaaahhhhh.*

WINCHELL: *A little more.*

JERRY: *Why so wide?*

WINCHELL: *So I can get in there.*

JERRY: *Hey, if you're gettin' in there, then I'm gettin' outta here!*

Among his many talents, Winchell was a successfully published songwriter and composed many of the songs used on his TV shows over the years.

represented security during the paranoid era of A-Bombs and McCarthy (Joe, that is—a character decidedly less fun than Charlie).

Between successful runs with his own programs, *The Paul Winchell-Jerry Mahoney Show* and *Winchell-Mahoney Time,* Winchell hosted several other similarly formatted shows for both NBC and ABC. The most notable of these was *Circus Time,* an hour-long show featuring the usual skits between Winchell and his dummies, along with circus acts from all over the world. Despite the hectic pace, fans put pressure on Winchell to make room in the spotlight for another cast member whose popularity would nearly eclipse both Winch and Mahoney: Knucklehead Smiff.

As soon as Jerry began reporting the antics of a certain unseen schoolmate, fan mail inquiries flooded into the studio with questions about the mysterious Knucklehead Smiff. As the letters began to pile up, Winchell's writing staff urged him to create a new puppet to fill the void. "I thought, 'Geez, what in the world would a kid named Knucklehead look like?'"

Using one of the unpainted Jerry Mahoney duplicates as a starting point, Winchell narrowed the top of the dummy's wooden head. "I tried to make it look like there wasn't much room for brains in there." Unlike Jerry, who had round, moving glass eyes and a wig, Knucklehead's eyes and hair were painted on, creating a simpler, less sophisticated character who needed help with just about everything, especially his math homework:

Kids loved the show. The duo embodied the classic father/son relationship that would so often appear on TV sitcoms in years to come—that sort of rascally son and understanding dad formula was integral to *Leave It to Beaver* or *My Three Sons.* There was only one distinct difference—the "son" in Winchell's world was a dummy. Still, the ventriloquist taught his little wooden boy the dos and don'ts of life, while conveying a sense of love, affection and security. And Jerry, like the other idealized children on TV in the 1950s, lived in a world where his primary concerns were the politics of Little League baseball, soapbox derbies and marble trading. Winchell and Mahoney's affectionate relationship reminded the audience that family and fun

After the tremendous success of Bergen and McCarthy a decade earlier, it was old hat to hear a vent on the radio by the late 1940s. Winchell and Mahoney, while traveling on the nightclub circuit, often found time for guest appearances on nationally and locally broadcast radio shows around the U.S.

WINCHELL: *Oh, Knucklehead, this problem is very simple.*

KNUCK: *'S that so?*

WINCHELL: *Yes, all you have to do is multiply by fractions.*

KNUCK: *By what?*

WINCHELL: *By fractions. You know what a fraction is don't you?*

KNUCK: *Oh sure. It's like that kid on the playground the other day.*

WINCHELL: *Now what does he have to do with a fraction.*

KNUCK: *Well, he broke his leg and the teacher said he had a fraction.*

Knucklehead—or Knuck, as he was often called—served the same function in Winchell's act that Mortimer Snerd had for Edgar Bergen: The dopey, well-meaning goof who was in direct contrast to the sharper witted McCarthy. But the dynamic between Jerry and Knuck is by no means an exact duplicate of Charlie and Mort. Winchell's wooden-headed comedy team was his homage to Bergen, a fond nod to an idolized legend.

Although Mortimer Snerd seems to be more of an adult country bumpkin, á la Disney's animated, guffawing Goofy, Knucklehead is in contrast the curious and not-very-bright child. Full of wonder and mischief and always well meaning, Knuck is the innocent simpleton.

Audiences adored Knucklehead Smiff and, like Jerry Mahoney before him, the charac-

In the early 1950s Knucklehead Smiff joined the Winchell-Mahoney act. The very popular character started out as a school chum of Jerry's and eventually became an adopted brother to Mahoney. It was never explained why Winchell and his two "sons" all had different last names.

ter's popularity compelled Winchell to produce more agile duplicate versions of the dummy. Knuck could soon clap, play the tambourine or throw a pie with the best of the day's TV comics. Knucklehead, his best pal Jerry and "Mr. Winkle," as Knuck often playfully called Winchell, soon became a trio of beloved pals for an entire generation of kids who grew up setting their Saturday morning alarm clocks to *Winchell-Mahoney Time.*

By 1963, Paul Winchell, like most of his vent contemporaries, was becoming part of a dying show business breed. When the network version of *Winchell-Mahoney Time* was cancelled in 1962, Winchell formed a partnership with Metromedia Inc., the owners of several independent TV stations around the U.S., to produce—on videotape and in color— new episodes of the show for syndication. Unfortunately, these new shows enjoyed only limited play on Metromedia's independent network and were never as widely received as Winchell's earlier NBC program. Though Winchell has continued his successful TV career as a voice-over actor for many years, his ventriloquial stardom and its effect on American culture is often forgotten. As TV producer Burt DuBrow, a close friend of Winchell's and a fan since his boyhood in the 1950s, puts it: "There never was and never will be another ventriloquist with more overall talent than Paul Winchell. He's the quintessential Renaissance man of early TV. It's amazing and sad that barely anyone knows who he his."

Part of the reason Winchell's work as a vent remains overlooked is that so few visual records of his performances remain. While some television shows from the pre-videotape era were produced on motion picture film, such as *I Love Lucy* and *Leave It To Beaver,* others were originally only intended for live transmission and were consequently unrecorded. However, some forward-thinking TV studios recognized the archival value of those live shows and, during the actual airing of the original broadcasts, photographed them directly onto film by aiming a movie camera at a television monitor. The resultant reels, known as kinescopes, were usually of poor quality. Most kinescopes ended up in the deepest recesses of studio vaults or were destroyed. Sadly, in Winchell's case, almost none of the kinescopes of his early work from the 1950s survive.

In 1972 Winchell attempted to retrieve the videotapes of hundreds of syndicated color episodes of *Winchell-Mahoney Time* made between 1963 and 1970, to which he owned half the rights. His plan was to explore the show's potential on the growing cable television market. A sixteen-year lawsuit ensued, during which it was revealed that the videotaped recordings of Winchell's later shows had been destroyed. The ventriloquist was awarded more than seventeen million dollars. The lawsuit set a precedent in the entertainment industry with regard to artists' rights, causing many in the industry to pay careful attention to film and video archiving and preservation, for legal as well as artistic reasons.

Winchell's legal victory was of little

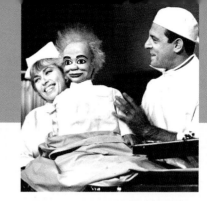

Is that Frankenstein or Einstein? Jerry gets a medical makeover in this late 1960s sketch, an homage to Bergen's humorous skit "The Operation."

from mr. winkle to dr. winchell

How many people know that an early proto-type for today's run-of-the-mill disposable razor was designed and patented not by an industrious barber named Mr. Bic but by a man most famous for playing with talking dummies? That same man is also a full-fledged doctor of acupuncture and has worked as a medical hypnotist. He can draw and paint, dance and sing, write and act and was into body-building long before Arnold Schwarzenegger made pumping iron a popular pastime. Want to swap ideas about the construction of a Web site? Ask Dr. Paul Winchell, ventriloquist, inventor and still Mr. Winkle to Knuck.

At least one of Dr. Winchell's innovations can be counted among the twentieth century's most monumental medical breakthroughs. That's right—a ventriloquist invented the first patented version of the artificial human heart.

Winchell's amazing, multi-faceted career defies belief. Frankly, it's difficult to imagine one man doing so many varied things so successfully in just one lifetime. The vent always dreamed of being a doctor, even as a teenager studying com-mercial art in 1936. Although Winchell had his first big break as a ventriloquist that same year on radio's *Major Bowes' Amateur Hour,* his love for ventriloquism never overshadowed his person-al interest in medicine and medical technology. Winchell's attraction to the field of medicine began at age six when he was stricken with polio. Although the young boy recovered from the disease, he was left with a noticeable limp, necessitating that he wear a special shoe.

Almost fifteen years later while perform-ing with Woody Herman's orchestra, Winchell met a member of the band who spent his free time exercising at local YMCAs while on the road, or—when no Y was available—with curtain

weights backstage at nightclubs. From then on, Winchell became fascinated with weight training. "I was an early version of one of those crazy body-builder guys," he says. More importantly, the ventriloquist was able to cure himself of his limp, beginning a lifelong fascination with the human body's ability to rebuild itself.

Another event occurred that sealed Winchell's involvement in the medical world. Early in the 1950s Winchell met Dr. Henry Heimlich, who would later gain fame for his life-saving Heimlich Maneuver to aid victims of choking. Heimlich quickly recognized Winchell's passion for medical science, and the two became good friends. "Dr. Heimlich was my mentor for many, many years. I even called him 'Hank,'" Winchell explains. Heimlich invited Winchell to observe many medical procedures, includ-ing heart operations. "I even helped perform autopsies," Winchell recalls. "My agent would call and say, 'What the hell are you doing at the hospital? We've got Hedy Lamarr here waiting to do a rehearsal!' and I'd say, 'Oh, my God, I forgot!' Nothing was more important to me than being at that hospital."

Winchell soon became interested in pain management and recovery. "I studied hypnosis and learned how to safely hypnotize people," he adds. "Before long, I was hypnotizing some of Heimlich's patients to help them deal with pain after surgery. I even taught Heimlich and his entire team of surgeons how to do it."

But Winchell's most important break-through happened because of a tragic event in 1955. "A friend of mine lost his little daughter to heart disease and I told Dr. Heimlich," Winchell recounts. "I thought that, if there could have been a unit standing by that could pump the blood for her, some artificial means that could

take over when her heart stopped, maybe there would have been time to save her. She might not have died." Heimlich encouraged the vent to, as Winchell put it, "jot down some ideas" for the artificial device he had in mind. "He said that he would be my devil's advocate and would let me know what he thought of my designs."

Winchell quickly went about producing models and drawings of a special "blood pump," and together with Heimlich devised what would become the first patented artificial human heart. "When I made that first heart, the valves in it were not widely different than the mechanisms that I devised to make Jerry Mahoney's eyes move," Winchell states. "What I learned from crafting puppets later helped me in the develop-ment of the artificial heart."

Winchell patented the artificial heart—which unlike later similar devices, required a power source outside the body—in 1963 and donated it to the University of Utah. Years later, another design, the Jarvik Heart, would make history as the first such device to actually be successfully implanted into a living human; such a feat which would not have been possible with-out the research from early pioneers in the field such as Paul Winchell and Henry Heimlich.

Winchell's medical interests never wavered. He became a doctor of acupuncture after graduating from the Acupuncture Research College of Los Angeles in 1974 and worked at the Gibbs Institute in Hollywood as a medical hypnotist. That same year, he was honored by National Christian University with an honorary doctorate in science for his innovation, invention and patent of the artificial heart. "For me, that artificial heart is the most important thing I've ever done," Dr. Winchell asserts. "I don't know where I'd be now if it had never happened."

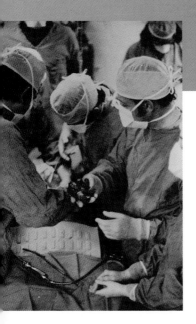

Fascinated all his life with medicine, Dr. Paul Winchell was the inventor of the first patented artificial human heart. In this 1971 photograph, he is shown (center with sideburns) assisting with an experimental veterinary procedure at the University of Utah.

FLIP = CLIP

comfort to his fans. Nothing can compensate for the loss of the programs, both as entertainment and as cultural record. Future generations will see few examples of Paul Winchell's genius as a ventriloquist, apart from the handful of grainy videotapes that sometimes turn up on Internet auctions or those that still manage to circulate among devoted collectors and enthusiasts.

Winchell continues to create memorable characters as a voice-over actor for famous cartoon characters such as Tigger from Disney's Winnie-the-Pooh franchise and Hanna-Barbera's Dick Dastardly from the *Wacky Races* series. These characters expose Winchell's comic genius to a new generation of children, but they don't portray the same amount of creativity, physical innovation and technical mastery that Winchell perfected on *Winchell-Mahoney Time* and *The Paul Winchell-Jerry Mahoney Show*. Together, Jerry and Winch taught an entire generation of children the value of good friends and inspired them to build relationships of their own. Those who remember Winch, Jerry and Knuck will never forget them—to do so would be like forgetting old school mates or childhood buddies. For true fans, their voices resound in the crackling hi-fis of our minds; their faces appear in the

black-and-white playbacks of our memories. Every episode of *Winchell-Mahoney Time* concluded with the song "Friends, Friends, Friends," written by Winchell and Hy Zaret:

Friends, Friends, Friends . . .

Whether in fair or in dark stormy weather.
We'll all stand—or we'll fall—together.
We're tried and true and we'll stick like glue.
In good times or bad times.
In happy or sad times.

We're friends, friends, friends.

This 1982 photograph shows sixty-year-old Paul Winchell with suitably aged versions of Jerry and Knucklehead posing to publicize a special "reunion" on TV.

DUMMY DATA

Flip Clip

NAME: TERRY MAHONEY/JERRY MAHONEY

ARRIVED ON THE SCENE: early 1936

DISTINGUISHING CHARACTERISTICS:
bore no physical resemblance to the famous Jerry Mahoney

Originally created at the School of Industrial Arts in Manhattan by fourteen-year-old student Paul Winchell, Terry Mahoney was the first incarnation of Jerry Mahoney. This dummy was the figure which Winchell used for his winning *Major Bowes' Original Amateur Hour* appearance.

FAMED REMARK: "Be more like you? And be good for nuttin'?!"

NAME: JERRY MAHONEY

ARRIVED ON THE SCENE: late 1937

DISTINGUISHING CHARACTERISTICS:
speaks Brooklyn-ese

While touring with the Ted Weems Orchestra, Winchell arrived in Chicago and asked famous dummy maker Frank Marshall to create a new figure for his Jerry Mahoney character. Marshall's Mahoney was able to move his eyes from side to side and wink with his right eye. The winking eyelid was made from a tiny strip of soft leather, a Frank Marshall trademark.

FAMED REMARK: "Hey, Winch, it looks like we're gonna eat tonight!"

NAME: JERRY MAHONEY

ARRIVED ON THE SCENE: 1950

DISTINGUISHING CHARACTERISTICS:
dislike of girls

Following his early appearances on Ed Sullivan's *Talk of the Town,* Winchell was signed to co-star on CBS's *The Bigelow Show.* Realizing that the new medium called for close-up photography, Winchell created a new Mahoney figure designed for TV. The new figure was greatly refined and outfitted with fully closing and rolling eyes, as well as ear holes that could squirt out smoke or water. Here Jerry also acquired Winchell's most enduring innovation—realistically moving arms, fingers and legs.

FAMED REMARK: "Scotty watty doo doo daa!"

Winchell introduced a number of hand puppets on the color, syndicated version of *Winchell-Mahoney Time*, including Snitchy the snail (who appeared as Jellybean on an episode of the classic *Dick Van Dyke Show* entitled "Talk to the Snail"), Irv Fink the educated mouse, Deauville the crow, and Scats the scarecrow.

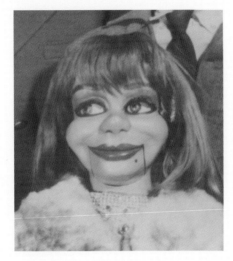

NAME: **KNUCKLEHEAD SMIFF (a.k.a. KNUCK)**

ARRIVED ON THE SCENE: early 1950s

DISTINGUISHING CHARACTERISTICS:

painted-on hair (Knuck was always jealous of Mahoney's full head of "real" hair and movable eyes), funny-shaped head, naiveté

After receiving a flood of fan mail inquiring as to the identity of Jerry's oft-mentioned but never-seen school chum, Winchell carved Knucklehead Smiff from an unfinished Mahoney dummy and added him to his growing cast of characters. Knucklehead was the vice-president of Jerry Mahoney's club on *The Paul Winchell-Jerry Mahoney Show*.

FAMED REMARK: "Mornin' Mr. Winkle."

NAME: **TESSIE MAHONEY**

ARRIVED ON THE SCENE: early 1960s

DISTINGUISHING CHARACTERISTICS:

looked a lot like Jerry, only with lipstick and a wig; sometimes a blonde; occasionally had auburn-colored hair

The flirtatious, raspy-voiced Tessie was an alleged cousin of Jerry's. When she joined the group, she stole Knucklehead's heart. Tessie appeared with Winchell on several TV shows in the late 1960s and early 1970s including *The Lucy Show* and *The Storybook Squares*.

FAMED REMARK: "Hiya, Doll Face!"

NAME: **HENRY JONES**

ARRIVED ON THE SCENE: around 1965

DISTINGUISHING CHARACTERISTICS:

also looked a lot like Jerry but was African American

Henry made guest appearances with Winchell on *The Della Reese Show* in the mid 1960s. However, the African American dummy never received the exposure that Winchell's other figures enjoyed. In the 1980s Henry changed his name to Goldberg, boasting that he was Whoopi's long lost cousin.

DANNY: *I resent that remark.*

NELSON: *Do you deny it?*

DANNY: *No, I just resent it.*

NELSON: *Be nice, Danny, or I'll put you down.*

DANNY: *Don't you always?*

FLIP=CLIP

jimmy nelson

Flip Clip

L ittle faces light up around the auditorium as Jimmy Nelson introduces his audience to Farfel, his puppet pooch. The elementary school children carefully watch the ventriloquist, captivated by the sweet, well-worn dog who can actually talk. Though they haven't guessed who's really doing the talking yet, the youngsters catch on to one thing instantly: Farfel is fun.

By the time this publicity photo was taken in 1960, Jimmy Nelson and his dummies were familiar faces on TV screens across America.

Of course, these children don't know that they are in the presence of two icons of American pop culture—but their teachers do. The star-struck adults in the room smile and laugh even louder than the students. Many of the adults, Baby Boomers who grew up watching Jimmy Nelson and his gang in those old Nestle's Quik commercials, could gleefully recite Farfel's famous jingle without falter. For those of us who grew up in front of the television set, seeing Farfel and Nelson again is like visiting with old friends.

Nelson soon brings out another dummy who receives a warm welcome from children and adults alike—the wisecracking, irascible Danny O'Day. With Danny on his right knee and Farfel on a table to the left, Nelson continues his act:

NELSON:	*Farfel, you don't smoke, do you?*
FARFEL:	*Don't be stupid. Did you ever see a dog smoke?*
NELSON:	*I guess not. Danny, you don't smoke, do you?*
DANNY:	*Of course not. If I did I'd burn to the ground!*

The vaudevillian patter is old shtick to Nelson, but to these kids it's all new. They listen intently. Though Danny's falsetto voice isn't as high as it used to be, it's clear that the

78

FLIP CLIP

Top dog Farfel, the crooning canine, became Jimmy Nelson's most popular dummy star.

semi-retired Nelson has still got it. He's able to deliver the anti-smoking message that is the real reason for today's volunteer performance on behalf of the American Lung Association— and make the children chuckle to boot.

Although American culture has changed much since the time when Jimmy Nelson and his comic partners were household names, the basic appeal remains the same. Children still love to see grown-ups cut down to their own size by creatures that they can relate to, whether human or not. Indeed, this humorous inversion is one of the many reasons why Nelson, Danny, Farfel and the rest of the gang were some of the most-watched television stars of the 1950s and 1960s. Viewers first became familiar with Nelson and Danny from their regular commercial skits on Milton Berle's highly popular *Texaco Star Theater* in the early 1950s, but the vent's celebrity status was solidified by a series of unforgettable Nestle's commercials that spanned a decade. Though the spots ran during every important time slot, Saturday mornings were perfect for reaching the young target audience. Indeed, at the peak of the ad's popularity in 1960, kids seemed more interested in Nelson's commercials than in many of the programs they sponsored.

Ironically, it wasn't Jimmy Nelson's talent as a ventriloquist that secured his spot in the Nestle's commercials, but rather, a technical mistake that experienced vents rarely make.

In 1955 Louis M. Cohen, Nelson's longtime talent agent, sent the ventriloquist to an audition for a TV commercial sponsored by Nestle's Chocolate Co. The commercial was a one-minute blurb for the instant chocolate drink mix, Nestle's Quik. Formerly, the spots had been sung in perfect harmony by western stars Roy Rogers and Dale Evans as part of *The Roy Rogers Show* and featured a simple, catchy jingle: "N-E-S-T-L-E-S, Nestle's makes the very best . . . CHOC-O-LATE."

Nestle's was looking for a new spokesperson to sing the same jingle. Since Nelson was already well known from *Texaco Star Theater* and his guest appearances on *The Ed Sullivan Show*, it made sense that the sponsor would want him. But he was still surprised to be the only ventriloquist called to audition for the spot. The director of the session handed him a copy of the song, asking the vent if he had any ideas for its presentation. "He didn't want the two-part harmony Roy and Dale had always done," Nelson explains. Lacking any specific direction, he improvised, using Danny to lead off:

DANNY: *N-E-S-T-L-E-S. Nestle's*
          makes the very best . . .

This was followed by the mournful, pinched-voiced Farfel, drawing the final word out for a big finish:

79

FARFEL: *CHAW-CLAAAAT!*

Just then the accident happened: Nelson was nervous and his sweaty finger slipped out of the trigger that worked the droopy dog's mouth. Farfel's mouth snapped shut, producing a loud, unexpected CLAP! at the end of the song. While the mishap elicited uproarious laughter from the executives and casting directors in the room, for Jimmy Nelson this sort of mistake was the ultimate no-no. One of the golden rules of ventriloquism is that the dummy's mouth should never clap, as it destroys the lifelike illusion. "I was mortified," Nelson recalls. "Farfel and I both walked out of there with our tails between our legs."

Much to Nelson's surprise, he was called back the next day. Relieved to be given a second chance, the eager young vent made sure that this time Farfel performed his part without a hitch. "I was proud of myself, until I heard the dead silence in the room." They were all waiting for the jaw snap they'd heard the day before and were disappointed when it didn't happen. "I had been a genius and didn't know it. They made me do it again, only with the clap." Thus, with a slip of the finger, Jimmy Nelson got the biggest break of his career—he became the spokesperson for Nestle's Quik for the next decade.

During the first year of Nestle's deal with Nelson, all of the commercials were produced live and continued to be presented on

The pitchman prowess of Nelson and his team, as well as The Lone Ranger, was Nestle's way of tantalizing retailers in the mid 1950s.

The Roy Rogers Show. The spots exhibited Nelson's prowess as a multi-tasking puppeteer: Each commercial featured Nelson standing before a table that was set with an empty drinking glass, a bottle of milk, a spoon and an open container of the chocolate drink mix. On the table to his right was Danny O'Day, with Farfel taking his customary place at the vent's left. After a bit of comic banter between the trio, Nelson would slip his hand from Farfel's hollow puppet neck to pick up the spoon and make a glass of chocolate milk. The one-handed maneuver was never detected, as Nelson made sure that his right hand kept Danny "alive," distracting the audience from Farfel's inactivity ("It helped that part of Farfel's personality was defined by his lack of movement," Nelson points out). This graceful ambidexterity, coupled with Nelson's quick voice changes, created a convincing illusion of three performers on camera. Occasionally, Nelson would up the ante even more by adding a third dummy, Humphrey

Higsbye, to the act. Given the physical impossibility of operating a third figure, Nelson used an extra puppeteer for Humphrey on these occasions, but he still managed, amazingly, to command all four voices at once.

Though the earliest spots might seem technically unsophisticated by modern standards, they clearly got the message across, and by 1956 Nestle's had expanded the advertising campaign to other television programs. Among these were popular hit shows such as *The Jackie Gleason Show* and *The Tommy and Jimmy Dorsey Show*. Nelson was present on one very historic installment of the Dorseys' show, when a young singer named Elvis Presley followed his Nestle's spot. "This was even before his famous censored *Ed Sullivan* appearance when they could only show him from the waist up. On the Dorsey show, the cameras showed him from head to toe, in all his wiggling glory. I like to think that, technically, Danny, Farfel and I were Elvis's first opening act on TV."

Before long, just about any TV viewer, regardless of demographic, could sing along with the Nestle's jingle—especially kids. Then in the late 1950s production methods for commercials changed from live broadcasting to film. With the freedom that film provided for multiple takes, Nelson and his sponsor could experiment with sets and scenarios. "Over the years, the Nestle's commercials became almost like little short films," Nelson explains. One innovative ad features the trio in the midst of an exciting auto race with Farfel at the wheel, Danny riding

For a brief time in the early 1980s, Nestle—no longer called Nestle's—brought back Farfel for TV ads promoting its chocolate drink mix.

81

shotgun and Nelson as their one-man pit crew. Of course, the refreshment of choice is a glass of Nestle's Quik. As the thirty-second spot nears its close, Nelson acts nervous:

NELSON: *Well, aren't you going to sing the song?*

DANNY: *No.*

NELSON: *Well, why not?*

DANNY: *Because the commercial's over.*

The screen abruptly cuts to black and, in a hilarious bit of disconnection, ends un-ceremoniously.

In another spot Nelson does an imper-sonation of Edward R. Murrow, the suave, cigarette-smoking journalist whose popular 1950 interview program was a precursor to shows such as *Larry King Live* or *Nightline*. In the Nestle's version, Nelson—cigarette and all—plays host to the famous Farfel, who appears on a large closed-circuit TV screen that is broad-cast "live" from a typical suburban kitchen:

NELSON: (doing his best Murrow) *Tell us Farfel, what is your favorite pastime?*

FARFEL: *Why, drinking delicious choco-late Nestle's Quik, of coooourse.*

A third commercial required Farfel to perform a spectacular ski jump. In case of injury to the dog, Nelson enlisted puppet maker Frank

Marshall to make a crude Farfel stunt double. This double was used for several years and kept the star of the series safe from harm. Today, Farfel's retired stand-in rests (miraculously, all in one piece) in Kentucky's Vent Haven Museum. (See "Where Have All the Dummies Gone?" on page 120.)

One of the most elaborate of the Nestle's commercials—and Nelson's personal favorite—was a special three-minute installment that involved a spaceship scenario. The spaceship is ready for takeoff, manned by Danny and Farfel,

This early 1960s photo goes behind-the-scenes of one of the more than 120 Nestle's commercials Nelson (far right) appeared in between 1955 and 1965. "We did a new one almost every month," Nelson said.

"BINGO!" Little did Aunt Margaret know that her bingo prize would spark a lifelong career for her nephew; Nelson is pictured here at age twelve in 1940 with Dummy Dan.

jimmy nelson

with Nelson serving as ground crew. After the two courageous astronauts pause for a drink of the sponsor's chocolate milk, the countdown begins. "Ignition! BLAST OFF!" yells Danny from the cockpit. There's a huge explosion, and when the smoke clears, the spaceship appears half buried in the launch pad:

DANNY: (with a nervous giggle): *Must have had the darn thing in reverse!*

Despite a successful run that spanned ten years, the inevitable happened in 1965: Nestle's decided to discontinue the Nelson campaign. The company informed the ventriloquist of its plans for a new pitchman, an animated rabbit. This news came as little surprise to Nelson; since the late 1950s, cartoons had increasingly begun to replace puppetry as the leading form of children's TV entertainment. Saturday morning programming, where Nelson's commercials had taken up primary residence, was altered according to the audience's newfound love for animation. The era of the puppet was over. But those individuals who remember Nelson's ads for Nestle's continue to treasure them. The imaginative spots captured the very essence of mid twentieth century American optimism—a gleeful spirit of innocent

adventure and fun. They endure poignantly as markers of a time when the future seemed prosperous and hopeful, full of jetpacks and singing dogs. All of this from a ventriloquist selling chocolate milk mix— not bad for a self-taught boy from Chicago.

Jimmy Nelson discovered his love for ventriloquism at a young age. Born in Chicago on December 15, 1928, he grew up during the heyday of Edgar Bergen and Charlie McCarthy's popularity. "My family and I would gather around the radio every Sunday night and 'watch' Bergen and McCarthy. Of course, so did just about everyone in America in those days." His father, James, was an accountant for the Eversharp Pen Co., while his mother Winifred made the home for James, Jimmy and his younger brother Donald.

When he was five years old, Jimmy contracted scarlet fever and was forced to undergo six months of treatment in an isolation ward at the Municipal Contagious Hospital of Chicago. Though his parents could visit daily, they were separated from him by a plate glass window. To keep their son occupied, his parents brought Jimmy a set of marionettes. Jimmy's interest in puppetry continued even after his recovery, and soon his talent became evident. As his brother Donald recalls, "Jimmy had natural

83

Flip Clip

Nelson had become a local Chicago celebrity by 1944. Here he poses with Dummy Dan, the toy his father modified into a more professional figure. The sailor suit on the dummy was hand made by the vent's mother. In his early performing years, Nelson appeared much younger than his actual age—here he is sixteen. To audiences he appeared to be a ventriloquial prodigy.

comic timing, even when he was a kid. On holidays, the whole family looked forward to little shows in the living room."

Just five years later Jimmy's Aunt Margaret won a toy ventriloquist's dummy at a church bingo game. Though disappointed in the prize, she remembered Jimmy's upcoming birthday. Dummy Dan was a perfect gift. And, as his aunt later said, "Jimmy turned the result of my bad luck into a career." Nelson took to the dummy immediately and called him Danny. The

on mr. bergen, a vent icon

Edgar Bergen was a gentleman of the first order. Soft-spoken and generous, he was willing to give professional advice to fledgling ventriloquists. My first meeting with him was in the early 1950s, when with fellow ventriloquists Stanley Burns and Clifford Guest, I went to catch his act at New York's Waldorf-Astoria Hotel. He was appearing in the famous Empire Room, and his act was class all the way. He graciously took time between shows to chat with us and even posed for pictures.

My biggest thrill, however, was yet to come. In 1958 on my opening night at the Mapes Hotel in Reno, I suffered an attack of

appendicitis. An urgent call was sent out to Edgar Bergen, who flew to Reno in his private plane to replace me for the duration of my engagement. He visited me at the hospital and I told him that I was absolutely in awe of having been replaced by my idol.

Our next meeting was at the dedication of a new wing of the Vent Haven Museum of Ventriloquism in 1973. The wing was dedicated to the museum's founder, W.S. Berger, who had collected ventriloquism memorabilia all his life. Edgar Bergen and I performed on a makeshift stage outside of the museum—he with Charlie McCarthy and Mortimer Snerd, and I with Danny

O'Day and Farfel. And, as usual, he graciously took all of the participants out to dinner after the show.

In 1978 we appeared together one last time for the HBO television special *The Vent Event*, which showcased established ventriloquists as well as up-and-coming talents.

It has always been an honor for me not just to have known Edgar Bergen, but to have appeared professionally with my inspiration, the icon of ventriloquism. He touched the lives of so many people, children and adults alike, in so many ways.

—JIMMY NELSON

Herman Stoike, whose stage name "Uncle Herman" is reflected in this autographed 1938 photo with his dummy Eddie, was Nelson's first vent tutor. Nelson and Stoike kept in touch until the teacher's death in the late 1950s

figure came with an instruction booklet consisting mostly of complicated diagrams explaining difficult tongue positions and diaphragm control, all of which proved too dull for an impatient ten-year-old ("After a while, I put the book aside and started teaching myself"). The aspiring ventriloquist sat in front of a mirror for weeks learning to talk without moving his lips.

Notice Danny's resemblance to young Nelson in 1950— a likeness purposely designed by puppet maker Frank Marshall as a surprise to the young vent.

He eventually gained enough confidence to take Danny to school for Show-and-Tell. The class loved it, and though he was a shy kid, Nelson's mind was made up—he was going to be a ventriloquist when he grew up.

Performances at school assemblies, churches and civic functions soon followed. Nelson, the ten-year-old ventriloquist, was a novelty hit. Soon the young vent found a mentor, Herman Stoike, a retired Chicago policeman and former vaudevillian performer. Once a week for the next year, Nelson and Stoike met for lessons. "Herman had a simple philosophy about the difficult letters. He advised me to avoid them." Nelson found that writing an entire routine while leaving out the sounds most difficult to pronounce (B, F, M, P, V, W and Y) was more of a challenge than training himself to actually say them. Still, Stoike taught Nelson two essential points that he would rely on for the rest of his career: First, that a ventriloquist's act has no more than five minutes to engage the audience, and second, the foremost thing that viewers look for is lip movement. "Once you pass the lip test, you'd better be funny or you'll die onstage," Stoike cautioned him.

Another ventriloquist, Bob Evans, took Nelson under his wing as well. Evans and his fast-talking dummy Jerry O'Leary performed in top-rated theaters and nightclubs. Following one of three matinees at the prestigious Chicago theater (all of which Jimmy had eagerly attended), Evans agreed to meet with the boy backstage. He encouraged Nelson to perform in

Nelson's mentor Bob Evans died tragically two years after this picture was taken in 1947 with his wooden partner Jerry O'Leary.

public as much as possible and even allowed the budding vent to stand in the wings during his evening show. As Nelson admits, "I wanted to be just like him. I even copied the falsetto voice he used for his dummy."

By age thirteen, Nelson started entering amateur talent shows with his family's full support. His father researched joke material, helped to customize Jimmy's dummy with a head stick made from a sawed-off broom handle, and even carried his son's suitcase to shows. Nelson's mother joined in by knitting clothes for Danny. Still only thirteen, the young vent won first place at a Chicago show called *Stars of Tomorrow*—the prize was five dollars and cab fare home. Winners were decided by audience applause, and the crowd wasn't afraid to boo bad acts off the stage. Nelson describes the experience as "the school of hard knocks, but that was where I cut my teeth in show business."

Within two years Nelson was a regular on a local radio program. An agent caught his act and offered the fifteen-year-old thirty-five bucks for a weekend-long stint at Chicago's Englewood Theater. Each weekend the theater presented a variety show featuring jugglers, magicians, crooners and dancers. "That first Friday night, I was terrified. But I looked a lot younger than fifteen, so the audience saw this little kid

In 1948, while living in Buffalo, twenty-year-old Nelson made one of his first TV appearances on a live local show called *Television Varieties*.

up there and that won them over." His performance was so well received that Nelson had trouble leaving the stage; the audience wanted an encore. "All I could think of to do was repeat a portion of the act I had just finished. But the audience ate it up."

Encouraged by his successes, Nelson decided he needed a better dummy, so in 1945 he met with the best: Frank Marshall. Renowned for his selectivity, Marshall proceeded to grill the teenager about his professional aspirations. The woodcarver insisted upon seeing Nelson perform before he would begin the job. "He showed up at my very next show. He must have liked it, because he called the next

At age twenty-four Nelson, along with his cast of dummies, became a star. "Everywhere I went, people would ask for my autograph," Nelson says. "I would have to sign both mine and Danny's names."

FLIP CLIP

day and said he would make me a figure." Nelson gladly cobbled together $125 for his new partner. The dummy had wavy brown, neatly cropped hair and red smiling lips that were slightly parted to reveal perfect white teeth and a hint of dimples on his rosy cheeks. He had a slight cleft in his chin and his bright brown glass eyes appeared lifelike—especially the right one, which could wink. The addition of a dapper scaled-down suit, shirt, bow tie and tiny leather shoes completed the ensemble. Since his vent heroes Edgar Bergen and Bob Evans had given their wooden sidekicks Irish-sounding names, Nelson named his new dummy Danny O'Day.

With new partner in hand, Nelson left Chicago after graduating from high school. He moved to Buffalo, the home of his high school sweetheart, Margot Humphries. The two were married in 1947 and soon became the parents of twin boys. With a family to support, young Nelson had to find work fast. Many of the Buffalo-area venues where he performed were tough, dilapidated joints: "Their idea of a dressing room was a broom closet with a nail in the wall. Professionally, it was probably my lowest time, but it taught me a lot about the tough realities of show business."

While difficult financially, Nelson's first years of performing with Danny O'Day were gratifying on an artistic level. Danny's rascally personality evolved on the job, and Nelson consistently delivered fresh material that he wrote himself. Sometimes billed as "The Mahogany Kid," Danny charmed the nightclub audiences by winking an eye or spinning his head around when he laughed. He would also flirt with the ladies, causing Nelson to scold Danny for his ornery antics and occasionally forcing the dummy to apologize. The illusion that Danny was real worked so well that once, when an intoxicated heckler took offense to the puppet's ad-libbed comebacks, the drunk threatened a violent retaliation: "I thought I was gonna get slugged. Then I realized he was going for Danny. Luckily, he was bounced out before he could do any damage, but the guy believed the dummy was real."

Just over a year after the move to Buffalo, the Nelson family returned to Chicago, where talent agent Louis M. Cohen took notice of Jimmy's act. Cohen, who booked variety acts into clubs and fairs throughout the Midwest, elevated Nelson's engagements from second-rate gigs to the big time. As Nelson's career grew, so too did his family. By 1949 he had three children. The road offered extra income, so Nelson began traveling almost constantly, doing one-night stands in top-rated supper clubs as well as regional radio and TV spots. It was a breakneck schedule, but the ventriloquist had been preparing his whole life for such an opportunity.

Danny, however, was beginning to show signs of over-work. So Nelson commissioned Marshall to create an exact duplicate of Danny O'Day as a backup. Unfortunately, he wasn't happy with the result. "It just didn't really look like Danny, but I didn't have the heart or the nerve, at age nineteen, to tell Frank that I wasn't a hundred percent satisfied." Since he had already paid for the misfit dummy, Nelson used the opportunity to create a new character. Outfitting the figure with nerdy spectacles, bushy black eyebrows, an oversized beret, sweater and jodhpurs, Nelson named the dummy Humphrey Higsbye, and took a third partner into his act.

In many ways Humphrey Higsbye became to Danny O'Day what Bergen's Mortimer Snerd was to Charlie McCarthy: a funny simpleton to a more quick-witted, savvy character. However, instead of emulating Snerd's country bumpkin, Nelson chose to give Humphrey a highly cultured voice. This new dummy eloquently rolled his R's and whistled his S's in similar fashion to veteran stage and screen actor Richard Haydn (the voice of the caterpillar in Disney's *Alice in Wonderland*). "Behind that Ivy League exterior, Humphrey was a dim bulb," Nelson remembers. "He never got any of Danny's jokes until the moment had long passed, then he would suddenly burst into

Aside from the Nestle's spots, Nelson and his dummies Danny, Farfel and Humphrey made guest appearances on TV shows such as *The Pat Boone Show* and *The Perry Como Show* throughout the 1950s. The vent also hosted one season of *Come Closer*, a quiz show, in 1954.

laughter. This always got Danny's goat, but Humphrey was oblivious. He got everything all wrong." This formula worked well for Nelson throughout the remaining years of the 1940s. His rapid-fire, three-way conversations with Danny and Humphrey established him as a master of quick voice changes and secured him a wider range of engagements, including television appearances.

At twenty-one years old, the vent began hosting a local show on Chicago's WGN-TV called *Holland's Happiness House*, sponsored by a local jeweler. Nelson arranged for a special guest appearance by his longtime mentor Bob Evans. The two performed a sketch in which Danny O'Day and Jerry O'Leary argue from opposing windows of a mock apartment building. As was often the case with live

FLIP ▼ CLIP

television, the episode was not taped, and a short time later Bob Evans was tragically killed in an auto accident. Another piece of vent history was lost forever. Jerry O'Leary now rests among the hundreds of other figures in the Vent Haven Museum.

Though it was Farfel who would one day bring Nelson his greatest renown, Danny O'Day was the figure that initially captured the hearts of a nationwide television audience. In 1950 Nelson's agent booked his act for a five-minute spot on *The Ed Sullivan Show*. After seeing Nelson rehearse for the show, Sullivan was impressed enough to praise the performer's technique in his on-air introduction, telling his viewers to "watch his lips. You won't see him move a muscle."

Fortunately, Jimmy Nelson's first Sullivan performance is preserved on videotape. Indeed, Sullivan was right—Nelson's lip control was amazing. The wisecracking Danny O'Day, wearing a suit to match Nelson's, seems to have a personality completely removed from his manipulator—the dummy does seem real. As Nelson casually lights and smokes a cigarette, Danny bounces to the beat and sings a lively falsetto version of "The Best Things in Life are Free." At one point the two trade voices, despite Nelson's protests:

NELSON: *I feel so silly.*

DANNY: *Well, you look so real.*
Now sing!

Ultimately, in order to silence the dummy, Nelson crams a handkerchief in his mouth, but the unshakable—though convincingly muffled—Danny keeps firing away the insults. Nelson takes Danny's barbs in stride, at times laughing along with the audience at his partner's ridiculous comments. Even during that first national TV appearance, there is a surprising element of sophistication in Nelson's act. Was he the first and only vent ever to incorporate the voice exchange bit or the hanky gag? No, endless variations on such material had been around since vaudeville, but Nelson's execution of these feats had elegance and charm. The element that set Jimmy Nelson apart as a ventriloquist was, and continues to be, the smooth, dancer-like grace with which he executes his craft. While Nelson addresses an audience, Danny's eyes slowly survey the room, his dummy head tilting and hollow body shifting in a very natural manner. When it comes to overall technique—lip control, puppet manipulation and quick voice changes—no ventriloquist has ever surpassed him. Nelson is a consummate professional. He is known as a ventriloquist's vent, a credit to his art form that both the trained and the untrained eye can enjoy. Though his work has been perfected over a lifetime, he makes it all as fresh as it was on his very first Sullivan appearance.

The year 1950 was a big one for Nelson. The same year that he hit it big on *The Ed Sullivan Show*, Nelson was offered a two-year spokesperson's contract hawking motor oil on

When Nelson and O'Day became the official pitchmen on Milton Berle's *Texaco Star Theater* in 1952, their ad spots were often tied into the live TV show's story line. Nelson often interacted with the show's guest stars, such as the Andrews Sisters and Ronald Reagan.

Flip Clip

Danny, Nelson and Farfel with Milton Berle on the set of the *Texaco Star Theater* in 1952. Though Berle was legendary as a demanding behind-the-scenes taskmaster, Nelson claims the experience was always pleasant. "It probably helped that I actually worked for the show's sponsor rather than for him."

Texaco Star Theater—the home of "Mr. Television" himself, Milton Berle. For the next two years, Jimmy Nelson was a regular on the live variety show, on which the host would often put on makeup or dress in women's clothing for a laugh. Halfway through each program, Nelson and Danny, each wearing gas-station-attendant uniforms, appeared in three-minute promotional skits for Texaco's automotive products. Often Humphrey Higsbye or Farfel would join in the sketches as well, which were usually written to include the evening's guest stars. Celebrities as diverse as the Andrews Sisters and Ronald Reagan interacted with Nelson and his figures. Of course, Berle sometimes got into the act as well:

BERLE: (to Danny)
          Listen you, not another word or
          I'll have you fired!

DANNY: (aside, to Nelson)
          Do you think he means it?

NELSON: *Yes, I think he does. You'd*
          better take him seriously.

DANNY: *That's hard to do.*

NELSON: *Why?*

DANNY: *Because five minutes ago he was*
          wearing an evening gown!

During his popular success on *Texaco Star Theater,* Nelson was offered his first chance to merchandise his characters. Danny O'Day (in a Texaco uniform), Humphrey Higsbye and

Farfel ventriloquist dolls and hand puppets soon appeared, manufactured by New York's National Mask and Puppet Co. A miniature cardboard Texaco service station replicated the set on the show. These toys, made briefly from 1953 to 1954, were never produced in large quantities, but they did enjoy brisk sales. A kid could have a Danny O'Day of his or her own, and the response was overwhelming. In fact, these early toy figures still remain in great demand—in the modern collectible market they fetch hundreds of dollars.

The young boy had certainly garnered show biz success, but not without cost. By 1951, the hectic schedule and stress of constant performance had brought an end to his first marriage. The young father and his three sons permanently relocated to Forest Hills, a community near New York City. With the help of a nanny, Nelson—a single parent and show business veteran at the age of twenty-four—continued his successful nightclub and TV acts.

If the first half of the 1950s was the period when Jimmy Nelson, Danny O'Day and

FLIP-CLIP

Humphrey Higsbye became TV stars, then the years between 1955 and 1965 could be referred to as "The Decade of the Dog." While Farfel had been occasionally featured on Berle's show, after his stint with Nestle's the pooch became top dog in Nelson's act—much to the ventriloquist's surprise: "I never dreamed that Farfel would one day become my most celebrated character. It was one of those unpredictable things."

Farfel's origin, like other breaks in Nelson's career, came through pure happenstance. During that pivotal year 1950, when he wasn't doing live spots on local TV or appearing on *Ed Sullivan,* Nelson continued to travel the nightclub circuit. One evening, during a late show at a small club in Wichita, Nelson confronted a particularly difficult audience. Realizing that his act was sinking and in need of something different, the ventriloquist spotted a small stuffed toy dog sitting on a nearby piano. Ad-libbing, Nelson grabbed the unclaimed plush animal and, using a sad nasal voice to contrast with Danny's falsetto one, worked it into the act:

DANNY: *You sure are an ugly looking dog.*

DOG: (deadpan, turning to Nelson)
           Oh, I wouldn't say that . . .
           Would yoooouuu?!

"It brought the house down. Of course, if a new bit works, you exploit it as much as you can. Looking back on it now, I wonder what would have become of me had that little stuffed dog not appeared on that piano back in Wichita."

Immediately upon his return to Chicago, Jimmy purchased a stuffed dog resembling the one he found at the Wichita club. He brought it to Frank Marshall, who then created a puppet in the plush toy's likeness: a seated basset hound upholstered in spotted, tan faux fur. His grinning wooden mouth opened wide to reveal top and bottom rows of shiny white teeth. A special lever in the puppet's hollow body allowed its long ears to prick up if desired. All in all, Farfel was a striking creation, possessing the simple elegance of American folk art characteristic of all of Marshall's best work. Nelson named the dog after a menu item he had seen while performing in the Catskills: farfel, meaning "little noodle."

Of course, after the debut of Farfel came the Nestle's campaign, and Nelson's already fast-paced professional life shifted into an even higher gear. So too did his personal life. In

In 1952 shortly after Jimmy Nelson began his regular appearances on Milton Berle's show, he returned to his hometown for a triumphant engagement at the Chicago theater and was greeted with a ticker tape parade.

Flip Clip

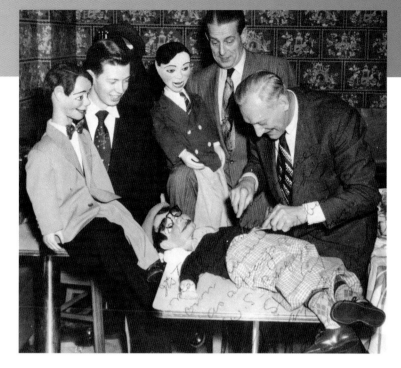

While visiting his hometown of Chicago in the late 1950s, Nelson (left, with Danny) catches up with friends, including Frank Marshall (right) and fellow vent Paul Stadelman (middle, with his dummy Windy Higgens). Marshall seems to think his creation Humphrey Higsbye needs surgery.

April 1956 Jimmy Nelson married Betty Norman, a young big-band singer he'd met while on the road and who, on occasion, had even joined him onstage for some comic ad-libbing. The couple soon increased their family with the births of two daughters.

As the 1960s progressed, Jimmy Nelson, Farfel and Danny O'Day became as recognizable on American television as other famed "pitch persons" such as Mrs. Olsen of Folger's Coffee or Comet Cleanser's Josephine the Plumber. So much so that in 1961 New York's Juro Novelty Co., famous for its toy versions of other celebrity ventriloquist dummies, Winchell's Jerry Mahoney and Bergen's Charlie McCarthy among them, began to produce retail replicas of Nelson's characters. Throughout the 1960s the popular Nelson Juro toys, including standard and deluxe versions of Danny O'Day and a Farfel hand puppet, were sold in stores across the country and prominently featured in the Sears, Roebuck

married to the magic

I met Jimmy Nelson in Minneapolis, when as a young singer, I was brought in to be his supporting act in the Flame Room of the Radisson Hotel. I was introduced to a rather shy, boyish-looking fellow I had only heard of through my booking agency. I was told that he was destined for great things and that if I was lucky, I could "ride in on his coattails." I had no idea of the enormity of his talent. Frankly, I wasn't fond of ventriloquist acts. It seemed the only thing the little figures ever talked about was their

allowance. That evening, as I watched Jimmy's performance from backstage, I was mesmerized by the way he handled himself and his dummies Danny O'Day and Humphrey Higsbye. All of those voices flying around, and the audience in the palm of his hand!

We worked together after and, needless to say, we got along very well and shared many exciting experiences—one of which was the birth of Farfel, that wonderful floppy-eared canine who has become an icon. Jimmy says that even

now people remember Farfel before they remember him.

Part of the success of Jimmy, Danny and Farfel is that Jimmy "thinks funny." Milton Berle once said, "In comedy you don't say funny things. You say things funny." Jimmy can even read newspaper headlines and make them sound funny. What a joy to spend my years with someone who is so much fun to be with.

—BETTY NELSON

FLIP=CLIP

and Co. Christmas catalog. The dolls, complete with beginner and advanced instructional records, went straight to the hearts of many kids of the era (this book's author among them). Juro was acquired by Goldberger Doll Co. in 1974 and, while the Farfel puppets have been discontinued, the Danny dolls—still produced from Juro's original molds—remain available and popular today.

After the Nestle's commercials ended in 1965, the ever-expanding Nelson family (a son was born in 1964) relocated to the coastal community of Cape Coral, Florida. "It came time to focus more on my family," says Nelson of the decision to move. Professionally, however, Nelson still traveled extensively, performing to enthusiastic audiences in clubs and at state fairs across the country. Many times throughout the late 1960s and early 1970s, the veteran vent, along with Danny and Farfel, revisited the Big Apple to co-host *The Mike Douglas Show* or appear on *The Merv Griffin Show*.

But Nelson understood show business well enough to know that the industry was constantly changing, and that by the 1970s, ventriloquism's years as mainstream entertainment were over. Beginning in 1972 Nelson appeared with his dummies in a series of short, regional TV ads sponsored by the Bank of Fort Myers, Florida. The commercials, scripted by Nelson, garnered much local popularity. As a result of this esteem, Nelson was named vice president of public relations for the bank, a job he happily held for eleven years until his semi-retirement in 1983.

Young, aspiring ventriloquists often approach Nelson these days to ask for advice. They are never turned away. Over the years, Nelson's peers have dubbed him "Gentleman Jim" because of his generosity in sharing old show business stories and tips on ventriloquism. Mark Wade, director of the Vent Haven International Ventriloquists Convention, refers to Nelson as "a living master of the art form. He influenced all of us," Wade acknowledges. "Jimmy's one of a very few people who really helped keep ventriloquism going longer than it might have. Without those Nestle's commercials or his Juro Danny dolls, kids growing up in the 1960s might have never been interested and there might not be any ventriloquists today."

Jimmy Nelson and Danny O'Day in 1964. Their lifelong partnership stands as a shining example of Nelson's natural talent, hard work and showmanship. "I've spent my life doing what I love most," he says. "I'm the luckiest guy alive."

93

DUMMY DATA

NAME: DUMMY DAN, DANNY DUM, DAN

ARRIVED ON THE SCENE: December 15, 1938

DISTINGUISHING CHARACTERISTICS:
fondness for bingo

Given to Nelson on his tenth birthday, this toy dummy was retooled by his father into a more professional figure. Nelson used this version of Danny until 1945.

NAME: DANNY O'DAY

ARRIVED ON THE SCENE: 1945

DISTINGUISHING CHARACTERISTICS:
high-pitched voice, neatly-cropped hair, rascally persona

Carved by Frank Marshall, Danny possessed the puppet maker's trademark right-winking eye. The falsetto-voiced O'Day would be Nelson's lifelong show business partner. After fifty-eight years—and still counting—Nelson still performs with this original Danny O'Day figure.

FAMED REMARK: "Timmm-BER!"

NAME: HUMPHREY HIGSBYE

ARRIVED ON THE SCENE: 1947

DISTINGUISHING CHARACTERISTICS:
black-rimmed glasses, beret, plaid knickers

Slow-witted Humphrey was originally meant to be a backup version of Danny O'Day. Nelson was dissatisfied with the new Frank Marshall-carved dummy's lack of resemblance to O'Day and decided to redress the figure, creating a new character. Humphrey enjoyed popularity during Nelson's early TV years, but was later eclipsed by Farfel the dog in 1955. By 1960 Humphrey was all but retired.

FAMED REMARK: "Lummm-BER!"

NAME: FARFEL

ARRIVED ON THE SCENE: 1950

DISTINGUISHING CHARACTERISTICS:

floppy ears, unforgettable singing

This lovable crooning canine was carved—again by Frank Marshall—and would go on to become Nelson's most enduring dummy star, best known for the famous Nestle's Quik television commercials. The puppet pooch provided constant torment to Danny O'Day and continues to make appearances with Nelson today, which makes Farfel almost three hundred and seventy years old (in dog years, of course).

FAMED REMARK: "CHAW-CLAAAAT!"

NAME: FTATATEETA (pronounced Fah-tot-ah-teet-ah)

ARRIVED ON THE SCENE: early 1960s

DISTINGUISHING CHARACTERISTICS:

feline whose grin could rival the Cheshire Cat's

Nelson commissioned Frank Marshall to carve this female cat character as a comic foil for Farfel. The coy Ftatateeta—whose unusual name is derived from one of Cleopatra's handmaidens—appeared in TV commercials for KEEN, a mid 1960s drink mix from Nestle's. Unfortunately, the dummy—whose voice sounded suspiciously like comic Ed Wynn—never caught on with audiences and has been hardly seen since then.

FAMED REMARK: "Ftatateeta. You don't PRONOUNCE it; you SNEEZE it!"

95

dummies for all

The Story of Juro Novelty Co. 1949-1977

Jimmy Nelson's Danny O'Day was Juro's top-selling toy dummy of the 1960s and was available in a variety of costumes.

If you're a Baby Boomer who had a ventriloquist doll as a child, chances are good that the Juro Novelty Co. made it.

And the great thing about vent dolls was that everyone, regardless of age or gender, played with them. "Ventriloquist's dummies were dolls that boys could play with, especially in the years before G.I. Joe came around," says Jimmy Nelson, who enjoyed success with dummy-doll versions of his Danny O'Day and Farfel characters. Though the first dolls based on Nelson's characters were made by the N.Y. Mask and Puppet Co., the vent formed a long-lasting relationship with Juro in 1961. There

were (and continue to be) many other toy vent doll manufacturing companies, but the Juro Novelty Co. is remembered today as the most prolific and successful maker of ventriloquist dolls and other vent-related toys ever. What began as a tiny New York City-based operation grew into an enterprise whose products left an indelible mark on the children of an era.

Sam Jupiter, a New York entrepreneur, established Juro Novelty Co. in 1949. The business began as a doll company. One of Juro's first retail successes was a line of child-sized "Dancing Dolls." These limber little mannequins were ingeniously outfitted with elastic

The kids pictured here and on page 99 all grew up to be professional ventriloquists.

Tom Ladshaw with Danny O'Day, 1972.

Conrad Hartz with Jerry Mahoney, 1955.

Dick Fitzmaurice with Jerry Mahoney, 1956.

FLIP CLIP

bands on the sole of each tiny cloth foot. When a real kid slipped these straps over his or her own shoes, the playful—and convincing—illusion of two dancing partners was achieved. (An adult-scale version of this same entertaining effect was adopted years later by vent Shari Lewis, who "danced" onstage with a faux Fred Astaire. Surely her inspiration for the clever bit originated from having owned one of these Juro dolls.)

Juro had the good fortune to emerge at the pivotal moment when TV was becoming an integral part of American life and was introducing fresh faces to the public daily. These new stars and their images were worth exploiting commercially. Well aware of this fact, enterprising Sam Jupiter moved quickly to produce a line of what he dubbed "Celebrity Dolls." The first of these was Dagmar, based on a now nearly forgotten character from the TV series *I Remember Mama*. Some time later came a toy version of kid's show host Pinky Lee (whose wacky character would

This 1979 trade ad for Juro, which by then had been acquired by Goldberger Dolls, best illustrates the craftsmanship that went into capturing a celebrity doll's likeness. The molds used to make these dolls are still in use today. Some, like Charlie McCarthy (center) and Danny O'Day (second from right), were originally sculpted in the early 1960s.

serve as a model for the future Pee-Wee Herman). Throughout the 1950s, Juro produced many television-celebrity-based dolls, but very few came close to the sales enjoyed by the company's vent-based merchandise.

Sam Jupiter wanted to reproduce the enormous success that the toy company Effanbee had over the previous two decades with its versions of radio's dummy star Charlie McCarthy. Unable to afford the likes of another Bergen doll, Jupiter offered a licensing opportunity to a young New York ventriloquist named Paul Winchell, who was just beginning to garner national attention with his own wise-cracking dummy, Jerry Mahoney. Jupiter envisioned a bright future for Winchell and secured a deal with him. Though the Jerry doll was originally a part of Juro's celebrity line, the figure had the added distinction of being the first of Juro's vent dolls.

By the mid 1950s it seemed that at least one kid on every block owned a Juro Jerry. Mahoney was Juro's best selling product throughout the decade,

In the mid 1960s, Sam Jupiter realized that his primary clientele were boys. Hoping to create a product that appealed to girls too, Jupiter collaborated with Jimmy Nelson to make Haley O'Hara, Juro's only female vent dummy. Meant as a toy girlfriend for Danny O'Day and one of the company's few dolls not patterned after an actual vent star, Haley never quite caught the attention of buyers and was soon discontinued.

97

Paul Winchell poses (back row, center) with a group of aspiring young vents. Four of the toy dummies pictured here are Juro Jerry Mahoney dolls. The bow-tied youngster second from the left is Jerry Layne, a Winchell protégé, who grew up to become a professional vent and leading figure maker.

Released in 1964 by Juro, the long-playing (and long-titled) record album *Jimmy Nelson's Instant Ventriloquism and Ventriloquism for the Beginner* graced the hi-fi set of many a young vent fan.

Juro Novelty Co. founder Sam Jupiter poses with Jimmy Nelson at the 1969 New York Toy Fair. The dolls at left and right are Danny O'Days, at center is a generic dummy "Little Ricky"—not connected to the TV son of lovable Lucy and Ricky Ricardo.

its success leading to the manufacture of Paul Winchell's other popular character, Knucklehead Smiff. The dolls secured Juro's position as the leading maker of toy ventriloquist dummies.

Around 1960, Paul decided to take back his license and produce his own toy versions of Jerry and Knuck. Luckily, Jupiter had a backup plan and soon two other dummy stars became part of Juro's Celebrity line: Jimmy Nelson's Danny O'Day and Farfel, the singing dog from the beloved Nestle's Quik commercials. Nelson's dummy duo became Juro's longest-running stars, staples in the Sears, Roebuck and Co. Christmas catalog throughout the 1960s and 1970s.

In 1967 Nelson recorded an instructional long-playing record called *Jimmy Nelson's 'Instant' Ventriloquism and Ventriloquism for the Beginner*—now a true classic within the vent niche—that became a must-have companion piece for all Juro dummy dolls. Fondly remembered by anyone who owned one, the album featured banter between Nelson, O'Day and Farfel, and presented simple instructions in the basics of vent art. On the flip side were various

mock routines with Nelson's dummies. The record made actually doing ventriloquism seem easy and accessible, and it sold like hotcakes. The LP's unprecedented success prompted Juro and Nelson to release another more advanced album the following year, which featured tips on stagecraft and dummy manipulation.

Over the course of the 1960s Sam Jupiter secured the rights to produce several other famous dummy-inspired dolls, finally getting the coveted licenses for Bergen's Charlie McCarthy and Mortimer Snerd as well. There was also vent Willie Tyler's Lester, who had gained fame on such TV programs as *Rowan and Martin's*

98

Laugh-In and *Hollywood Squares*. Curiously, during the same period Jupiter created dummy dolls of some non-vent human celebrities, such as Groucho Marx and sad clown Emmett Kelly. Despite the seemingly incongruous concept of these dolls, both enjoyed strong sales.

At the time, other companies that produced toy ventriloquist dolls had strong sales too—most notably Horseman Dolls, which made versions of Howdy Doody and Mickey Mouse—but Juro dominated the dummy market. Sales were showing no sign of slowing when in 1974, after a long period of failing health, Sam Jupiter died. For a brief time, his wife Miriam stepped in to oversee Juro's production, soon handing over the reins to her daughter and son-in-law, Vivian and Victor Spetalnick.

In 1977 Goldberger Dolls acquired Juro Novelty Co., the little doll-making shop Sam Jupiter had turned into the leader in its field. Juro's original molds for Danny O'Day, Charlie McCarthy and Mortimer Snerd still serve as the bases for Goldberger's versions of those classic vent characters. Companies such as J.C. Penney and mail order giant Johnson-Smith carry the dolls year round. The lasting appeal of a Juro dummy doll is a testament to the impact of ventriloquism on American culture and to the enterprising skills of Sam Jupiter.

"Sam loved his work," Victor Spetalnick says. "He would be amazed and thrilled that people remember Juro's dolls as such a big part of their childhoods."

Danny O'Day as Uncle Sam.

Bruce Weaver with Jerry Mahoney, 1962.

Pete Michaels with Danny O'Day, 1965.

Michael Eakins with Jerry Mahoney, 1959.

frank marshall (1900–1969)

America's Forgotten Geppetto

I f the United States were a nation populated primarily by ventriloquists, Frank Marshall's face would surely grace its currency. No single individual did more to influence the art of ventriloquism as popular entertainment in America, touching the lives of many professional vents who went on to great success. He made the dummies that these vents magically brought to life. Many of Marshall's creations went on to great fame: Danny O'Day, Jerry Mahoney, Farfel—these characters epitomized his distinctive style. Fans can recognize a Marshall dummy anywhere: the heavily lined eye, the smiling "cheeky boy" features. These are the characteristics of the classic ventriloquist dummy.

Born in Chicago in 1900, Marshall grew up loving puppetry and ventriloquism. Because he was crippled with polio as a child, young Marshall chose the sedentary activity of woodcarving as a hobby. By age fourteen, his skills were good enough to land him a job at the local furniture factory of Theodore Mack and Son, where puppets were also produced. Most notably among the shop's creations was Edgar Bergen's version of Charlie McCarthy, the dummy with which the vent would attain great fame. Charlie's beginnings are the source of great—and at times heated—debate among veteran vents: Did Frank Marshall carve the first Charlie McCarthy or didn't he?

Frank Marshall is on record stating that his employment with the Macks began in 1914. He would indeed have been working at the shop at the time of Charlie's 1922 "birth." It is documented that Theodore Mack assigned Marshall the regular task of producing stock wooden dummy and puppet heads, which were subsequently customized, depending on a given client's requests. It is also well known that Edgar Bergen personally drew sketches of the newsboy character he desired, presenting the drawings to Mack when he ordered the new dummy. Some speculate that Charlie's face and head may have originated from one of the shop's existing standard dummy heads, and that Bergen's drawings determined his unique look. Thus, it is indeed possible that the stock head used was one among the many produced by Frank Marshall. In the eighty-plus years since Charlie McCarthy was carved, many

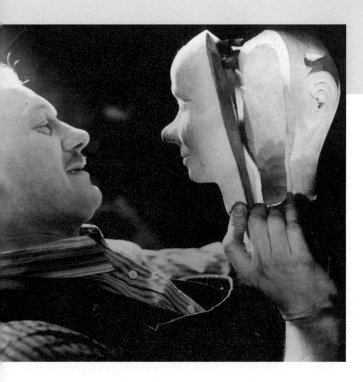

FLIP CLIP

Marshall inspects an unfinished dummy head in this beautiful undated photo of the famed puppet carver.

sources have gone so far as to quote Marshall himself claiming credit for the creation of the wooden-headed icon. However, others, who knew the famed woodcarver, say he denounced such statements.

Marshall purchased the Mack's shop in 1927 and over the next four decades until his death in 1969 produced thousands of puppets for entertainers nationwide. In the late 1930s he was the original carver of the character Jerry Mahoney for a young vent named Paul Winchell and, in the 1940s, the characters Danny O'Day, Humphrey Higsbye and Farfel for Jimmy Nelson. Even such unlikely celebrities as the *Tonight Show* host Johnny Carson, a ventriloquist early in his career, owned a Marshall figure.

Once Marshall's creations sold for as little as thirty-five dollars; now these same figures command many thousands at auction. Some of Frank Marshall's dummies have even

made their ways into museums, including the Smithsonian Institution, where his original version of Winchell's Jerry Mahoney is part of the permanent collection.

"Frank Marshall is the figure maker's figure maker," says Mike Brose, a professional ventriloquist and author of *Figure Making Can Be Fun?!?* (Puppets and Props Press, 2001), "That's why so many figure makers have tried to emulate his style." Brose's fellow ventriloquist and figure maker Ray Guyll, who for years has repaired and refurbished Jimmy Nelson's original Marshall dummies, agrees: "Marshall was a genius who was right for his time. He was largely responsible for that Golden Age of ventriloquism. He created characters who became beloved by generations of people."

Just to look at the faces of Danny, Farfel, Jerry and the many appealing dummy faces Marshall created is to observe the work of a true American folk artist. Indeed, a real-life Geppetto.

Backstage at the popular Chicago nightclub Pepe's in 1963, Frank Marshall (left) and friend, vent Bob Isaacson (center), visit between shows with Jimmy Nelson and his cast of Marshall-made dummies.

101

LAMB CHOP: *Ah, what a cute D-O.*

SHARI: *D-O?*

LAMB CHOP: *Yeah, D-O. That's how you spell DOG!*

SHARI: *Oh . . . but isn't there something on the end?*

LAMB CHOP: *Oh yes . . . a TAIL!*

FLIP-CLIP

shari lewis

Flip Clip

Shari Lewis, shown here in 1956 with sock puppets Lamb Chop (left) and Charlie Horse on the set of *Shariland* (note the cardboard castle in the background), her locally broadcast New York children's show.

This 1960s publicity portrait captures the fresh-faced "Big Sister" that Shari Lewis personified in her early years on TV. Her cheerleader-like enthusiasm and extraordinary talent propelled her through decades of stardom.

In the late 1950s, while soon-to-be First Lady Jacqueline Kennedy was just beginning her ascent into legend, another multi-talented and charismatic woman was rising to prominence, albeit in a very different field. In the eyes of ventriloquists and the children who watched them, Shari Lewis became the First Lady of puppeteering, and like Jackie Kennedy, she emerged as a symbol of the era's shifting ideas about gender, power and performance.

Lewis influenced the Baby Boomer generation, teaching boys and girls alike that females were every bit as clever as their male counterparts. Again like Jackie Kennedy, her style was instrumental in getting American kids (and their parents) to pay attention. As an ingénue, Lewis had everything going for her-- her ponytailed hair, boundless energy and pixie face corresponded to the current Hollywood mold of the screen's biggest stars such as Doris Day, Julie Andrews and Natalie Wood. Before the Age of Aquarius, these young women were role models and the squeaky-clean face reigned. Americans embraced this new notion of womanhood as youthful, optimistic and, in a word, perky.

As a singer, dancer, writer, musician and ventriloquist, Lewis fit right into the larger context of the changing role of women within the entertainment industry, proving that a woman practicing an art form once dominated by men could be innovative and enduringly popular. During the course of her career, she starred in ten of her own television shows, won twelve Emmy awards and authored more than sixty children's books. But most important for the kids who grew up watching her, Shari Lewis transformed an old sock into a lovable, enduring puppet superstar.

When her big break came to appear on the nationally televised *Captain Kangaroo* show in 1957, the only caveat was that she couldn't perform with her usual dummy, Samson. Bob Keeshan, the host of *Captain Kangaroo*, and the show's producers thought wooden dummies were old hat. Couldn't the up-and-coming ventriloquist get a new partner, and fast? Perplexed, Lewis suddenly remembered the gift her father had given her years before. He had presented it—a sleepy, white lamb sock puppet— to his daughter with the quip, "If Mary had a little lamb, why shouldn't Shari have one too?"

Lewis in 1953, demonstrating what she called "Balloonimals," one of the many bits featured in the live shows she performed at birthday parties, civic functions and amateur shows early in her career.

At the time, the fleecy puppet didn't interest the young vent and she relegated it to a shoebox, where the little lamb lay forgotten among the dust bunnies of her room. But out of that shoebox came the legendary Lamb Chop.

Lewis, like her Lamb Chop, came from humble beginnings. Born Phyllis Hurwitz (though she decided at a young age to change her name to Shari) on January 17, 1933, she grew up in the Park Chester Housing Projects of New York City's East Bronx. Young Shari inherited a love for performing from her talented parents. Her mother, Ann Ritz Hurwitz, an accomplished musician, was music coordinator for the New York public schools.

She home-schooled her daughter at the piano and violin, and enrolled Shari in ballet and art classes, determined that her little girl would always have an appreciation for the arts. Abraham Hurwitz was a professor of education at Yeshiva University and was also a professional magician who became well known in the city as "Peter Pan the Magic Man." Abraham was so active in the community that his friend, Mayor Fiorello LaGuardia, bestowed upon him the honorary title of "Official Magician of New York City." His teaching philosophy was that children learn more when they are having fun in the process, and to the delight and benefit of his daughters, Abraham used that same philosophy at home. Shari and her younger sister Barbara lived in a child's wonderland, full of music, art, magic tricks and puppets. What more could two little girls want?

"Peter Pan the Magic Man," as Lewis's father, Abraham Hurwitz, was known, taught his daughter magic tricks. Later in the 1960s, Lewis and her dad co-wrote several activity books for kids.

105

Lewis, pictured here circa 1945, had a natural grace that was evident in everything she attempted, which led to her enrollment at New York's esteemed Music and Arts High School.

Even at the age of ten in 1943, Lewis was poised for show biz victory.

No wonder, then, that Shari Hurwitz became a neighborhood celebrity before she reached high school age. She could play the violin (or fiddle, depending on the occasion), guitar, piano and trumpet, and could manage a tune on several other instruments. The precocious girl effortlessly shifted from ballet to tap to modern dance to the construction of balloon animals while her audience cheered her on. With Shari's unquenchable thirst to learn new performance skills, it was only a matter of time before she discovered ventriloquism.

The story of how she started has become vent-world legend: One evening in the Hurwitz apartment, probably around 1945 when Shari was twelve years old, Abraham heard his daughter Barbara calling from a locked broom closet. Rushing to free her, he flung open the door only to discover it empty. Nearby, Shari giggled. Even her father, a master magician, was fooled by the girl's latest trick. Shari had nurtured her new talent almost in secret, under the tutelage of a retired African-American ventriloquist named John Cooper, whom she had met in the park. Cooper was a top vaudevillian theater performer in his day, and by the time Shari met him, the old pro was well into his eighties. Cooper would occasionally treat the local playground kids to an impromptu show in the park with his dummy, Sam. Those skits clearly provided Lewis with inspiration. Soon Cooper began giving interested youngsters a few pointers. Shari caught on faster than the other children, and demonstrated a particular talent

for ventriloquism, which she would always attribute to a natural ability. The chance meeting of John Cooper and his subsequent mentoring opened the door to the inevitable: Shari Lewis was going to become a vent.

Proudly, Abraham Hurwitz bought his daughter her first professional dummy, the classic-style, wooden, slotted-mouth figure, which she named Samson. Shari developed his character into a stereotypically high-strung talent agent, dispensing career advice and constantly on the prowl for the Shari's next paying gig. For added effect, Samson could, through the clever use of a rubber tube and squeeze bulb hidden in his hollow torso, smoke a cigar which fit snuggly into his specially designed mouth. (Unfortunately, all that remains of Samson today are fragments of old TV footage and a few faded publicity photos.) There were also other wooden dummies incorporated into Shari's act, including a girl character named Taffy Twinkle and her brother Dinky.

Throughout her teens, Shari attended New York's Music and Art High School (the same

Shari Lewis in 1952 with her first
ventriloquist dummy, Samson.

school made famous by the 1980 film and subsequent TV show *Fame*). During evenings and weekends she performed ventriloquism acts at local community centers and variety shows. Teachers, classmates and audiences alike recognized her energy and charisma onstage and agreed that they were witnessing a talent for which show business success seemed inevitable. Shortly after graduating from high school, Shari was briefly married to Stan Lewis, whose surname she would use professionally for the rest

Publicity photos such as this one from 1951 show
that Lewis had another dummy named Buttercup.
The toy monkey's identity remains a mystery.

of her life. By 1952 the divorced nineteen-year-old Shari Lewis, already a seasoned professional ventriloquist, was at the threshold of fame.

The early days of television offered, for the first time, the chance for fans to see rather than just hear their favorite radio stars. Hence, many radio programs successfully made the transition to TV's visual realm. One of the most popular programs to make the switch was *Arthur Godfrey's Talent Scouts,* which ran on CBS's Monday night lineup. Godfrey had a laid-back, self-effacing style that was extremely popular with audiences in the 1950s. Though the program was billed as a variety show, it consisted mostly of unknown performers looking for that big break and, in a few cases, that's exactly what resulted. Enduring legends such as Tony Bennett, Lenny Bruce and Patsy Cline received early notice after their appearances on Godfrey's show. With her ambitious father's help, Lewis secured an audition for *Talent Scouts* and was immediately selected to appear. The program always ended with a vote from the studio audience via an applause meter to determine the evening's winner. On the night she appeared in 1952, Lewis won first place. The young vent was a hit.

In 1953 Lewis was offered her first recurring television spot in a series of educational programs produced by a local New York station. *Facts 'n' Fun with Shari Lewis* aired on a fifteen-minute slot between cartoon programs on

Like Señor Wences, Lewis
was a master of the "distant
voice," and incorporated the
technique into her early act.
In this 1950s publicity shot,
Lewis's stalwart talent
agent Samson takes a call.

Lewis with one of her earliest dummies, Taffy Twinkle, in 1954. Used as part of an ad campaign for Air France, the executives who found Lewis certainly made a smart decision; she was definitely a young woman on the move.

The title of this 1954 New York trade paper demonstrates the transition from radio to television, and showcases a few fresh-faced performers on its cover. Shari Lewis (center) and Alan Ludden (left) would both find success on the new medium, Lewis in children's programming, and Ludden as the host of the game show *Password*.

Sunday mornings. Each live installment featured Lewis and her characters performing for a studio audience filled with kids. Lewis, Samson and Taffy told stories, sang songs, conducted celebrity interviews and, most importantly, stated interesting facts about subjects ranging from animals, science and history to math, art and astronomy. Lewis used the same method her father had used in schools: fun coupled with learning. The following year Lewis was offered another TV spot as the host of the similarly formatted *Kartoon Klub*. Though this show had several incarnations and titles over time, it garnered Lewis genuine celebrity—at least in New York. By 1955 the show (then titled *Shari and Her Friends*) had caught the attention of Bob Keeshan, the host of a new nationally broadcast children's show called *Captain Kangaroo*.

Before he became the Captain, Bob Keeshan starred in another children's program, playing Clarabell the Clown on *The Howdy Doody Show*. Airing on weekday mornings from 1955 until 1993, the ninety-minute *Captain Kangaroo* show was tailor-made for early-rising preschoolers, gently educating and entertaining them while busy parents prepared for the day. With no violence, villainy or potentially nightmare-inducing elements, *Captain Kangaroo* became the kids' show parents trusted most. Set in a magical room known as the Treasure House and presided over by Keeshan as the mustachioed and uniformed Captain, the show featured several lovable puppets. The sleepy, kindly Grandfather Clock never knew the correct time, the confident

Mr. Moose collected ping-pong balls, and his rival, mischievous Bunny Rabbit, was fond of dropping bunches of straw on unsuspecting guests. These puppets interacted with human characters, such as the famous animal and agricultural expert Mr. Green Jeans, who often showcased one of his exotic pets, such as a baby spider monkey or trained raccoon cub. There was the enterprising and comical mime, the Town Clown, who lived on the outskirts of the village in his broken-down circus trailer. The most memorable of all was the costumed Dancing Bear, who could fashion an imaginary

FLIP CLIP

partner from a coat rack or broom handle and waltz it about the room with the grace of Fred Astaire. These quirky characters, along with special guests from all walks of life and ethnicities, came together to create what, by today's standards, amounted to *Good Morning America* for kids. The far-reaching influence of the show is evident on many of the kids' shows that followed, such as *Pee-Wee's Playhouse* and the long-running *Mr. Rogers' Neighborhood,* which owed much to the format of *Captain Kangaroo.*

A show like the Captain's was perfect for a talent like Shari Lewis. Lewis knew this, so she was thrilled when Keeshan asked her to be a guest on the show despite the stipulation that she couldn't bring Samson along. Rather than panic, the twenty-two-year-old eagerly took the opportunity to introduce a new character, the playful and sometimes exasperating Lamb Chop.

From the beginning, Lewis had her little sock puppet's characterization fully developed. Lamb Chop was a precocious, inquisitive, six-year-old female, with a high-pitched voice and a Brooklyn accent. In Lamb Chop's perpetually preschool world, there was always wonder, discovery and acute curiosity. And, like regular little lambs, she could be a little bratty:

LAMB CHOP: *Knock, knock.*

SHARI: *Who's there?*

LAMB CHOP: *Who.*

SHARI: *Who, who?*

LAMB CHOP: *What are you, an owl?*
(Followed by uncontrollable laughter.)

SHARI: *Oh, Lamb Chop, that's silly.*

LAMB CHOP: *I know, and it's funny, too.*

Like most children, Lamb Chop greeted new experiences with a barrage of questions. She could tell a joke and giggle with delight, proud of her own astonishing wit, or she could defiantly pout over not getting her way. Most importantly, everything in Lamb Chop's experience resulted in subtle lessons learned, be they in simple math problems or in tying a shoelace:

LAMB CHOP: *Hey, Shari.*

SHARI: *Yes, Lamb Chop?*

LAMB CHOP: *I've decided something.*

SHARI: *Oh? And what is it that you've decided?*

LAMB CHOP: *I've decided that I like my socks better than my shoes.*

SHARI: *I see. And why is that?*

LAMB CHOP: *Because my socks never end up on the wrong foot.*

The introduction of Lamb Chop on *Captain Kangaroo* was a hit, and by 1955 Shari Lewis was a definite success. Her local New York show continued to be popular and was re-titled as *Shariland* in 1956. *Shariland* featured Lamb

A not-so-distant cousin to Señor Wences's Johnny, Thumbkin was featured in a 1950s magazine article in which Lewis provided instructions for making simple puppets.

109

Chop and a cast of other new sock-based pup-pets—Lewis would never again utilize traditional wooden, ventriloquist dummies. And why should she? She was beginning to develop her own approach to the traditional vent world:

SHARI: *Now Lamb Chop, have you finished your ABCs?*

LAMB CHOP: *Yes, and all the other letters, too.*

SHARI: *Oh that's very good.*

LAMB CHOP: *And they were delicious.*

SHARI: *Delicious?*

LAMB CHOP: *Yes, alphabet soup is my favorite.*

Charlie Horse, a freckled, bushy-maned, buck-toothed equine, was one of the new plush personalities who joined Lewis's cast of characters. Energetic and street smart with a voice slightly reminiscent of an early Bugs Bunny, Charlie Horse was definitely big brother to the rest of the gang:

CHARLIE HORSE: *I've decided what I want to be when I grow up.*

LAMB CHOP: *Oh, really? And what's that?*

CHARLIE HORSE: *An adult.*

Though she was petite in stature, Lewis's influence was gigantic. No other female ventriloquist has come close to reaching the fame she attained.

Along with the savvy horse, Lewis added another character, a floppy-eared dachshund named Hush Puppy. Whether the doe-eyed pup was named for the famous line of boy's shoes or the delicious fried side dish is not known, but the character's southern accent favors the second theory. Always caught in the verbal crossfire between the lamb and the horse, Hush Puppy assumed the role of the middle child among Lewis's gang of cushiony characters:

CHARLIE HORSE: *Hey, which one of you left an egg in my chair?*

LAMB CHOP: *Not me.*

Lewis and Charlie Horse, shortly after the vent's success in 1955 unveiling Lamb Chop on *Captain Kangaroo*. Lewis's ability to sing lively, three-way songs with her characters quickly placed her among the ranks of TV's best ventriloquists, such as contemporaries Paul Winchell and Jimmy Nelson.

FLIP ▼ CLIP

HUSH PUPPY:	*Me neither.*
CHARLIE HORSE:	*Well, someone had to have left it there.*
HUSH PUPPY:	*Maybe it was the Easter Bunny.*
CHARLIE HORSE:	*But it's not Easter.*
LAMB CHOP:	*That's true.*
CHARLIE HORSE:	*Well, whoever left it there is in big trouble.*
HUSH PUPPY:	*Why is that?*
CHARLIE HORSE:	*Because I sat on it.*
HUSH PUPPY:	*Oh . . . Well . . . I guess that means the YOLK's on you!*

The hour-long *Shariland* was a memorable program, and the show won multiple Emmy awards in 1957 for both best female performer on a children's program and best children's show. *Shariland* treated young Saturday morning viewers to lively songs, stories and short films that dealt with subjects ranging from wildlife to the solar system. Soon the local network offered Lewis an additional weekday morning program called *Hi Mom!* which also featured Lewis with her expanding cast of fleecy puppets, talking to mothers who watched along with their kids. In a truly innovative move, Lewis took the opportunity to teach mothers how to interact with their children (long before the term "quality time" had been coined).

Doing both *Shariland* and *Hi Mom!*

meant Lewis appeared in six hours of television a week, a busy schedule that demanded the memorization and rehearsals of dozens of songs and skits. Exhausting, even for the energetic Lewis. But her efforts were rewarded in 1958 when *Hi Mom!* won two Emmys in the same categories that *Shariland* had swept the previous year. All of these experiences, however, only served as preparation for even greater success to come.

While Lewis's professional life was moving at a breakneck pace, so too was her personal life. In 1958 she married Jeremy Tarcher, at the time a young New York television studio executive who would later establish a successful publishing firm. From the start they were a bright, dynamic couple; they would

Hush Puppy was created contemporaneously with Charlie Horse and enjoyed equal popularity with young TV audiences. For a time in the mid 1960s, Lewis and her husband Jeremy Tarcher produced popular toy replicas of Lewis's sock puppet trio. Today, the rubber-and-cloth puppets are sought-after collector's items.

Flip Clip

Shari's natural beauty was never more evident than in this 1958 bridal portrait.

enjoy personal and professional success, both together and individually, for the next forty years.

The exposure that Lewis received from her *Captain Kangaroo* appearances led to guest spots on other nationally televised shows such as *The Jack Benny Show* and *The Ed Sullivan Show.* While her material for these adult venues could venture beyond the realm of children's education, the core ingredient of her act—clean-cut, warm-hearted humor—never wavered. This clever, funny, girl-next-door image was the Shari Lewis her fans knew and loved.

In 1960 Lewis got her biggest break— NBC offered her the time slot once held by the beloved American pop icon, Howdy Doody. Though out of style with viewers by that time, *The Howdy Doody Show* had been a fixture on the network since 1947. The opportunity to create another show in its place was a golden one, but the petite young Shari Lewis certainly would have some very big cowboy boots to fill.

Beginning on October 15, 1960, for an hour every Saturday morning, kids tuned in to NBC to watch *The Shari Lewis Show.* Lamb Chop, Charlie Horse and Hush Puppy were like the rowdy kids who lived next door, complete with tree house, tire swing and knot-holed picket fence. It was a setting that felt comfortable and familiar to the growing American middle class now living in the suburbs. The show centered on Lewis's constant attempts to keep peace among her puppets and a variety of wacky neighbors played by such great comic actors as Dom DeLuise, Fred Gwynne and Margaret Hamilton

(who had played the wicked witch in the 1939 film *The Wizard of Oz*), among others. Each week's show had a different educational or moral subject, based on simple themes such as Charlie Horse's fear of having to apologize after breaking a window, or Hush Puppy's first day of school.

Whatever the lesson, humor was the sweetener Shari Lewis used to make learning more palatable for kids. For example, a skit in which Lamb Chop was feeling anxious about being liked would never hit the viewer over the head with the intended message but would deliver it through lighthearted banter:

LAMB CHOP:	*Oh Shari, please don't open the birthday present I gave you.*
SHARI:	*Well, why not?*
LAMB CHOP:	*What if you don't like it?*
SHARI:	*Oh, don't be silly, of course I'll like it.*
LAMB CHOP:	*How do you know?*
SHARI:	*Well, because I'm sure I'll like anything you give me.*
LAMB CHOP:	*Even if you don't open it?*
SHARI:	*Yes, even if I don't open it.*
LAMB CHOP:	*Good, then don't open it.*

Lewis entertained and taught at the same time, delighting her young audience. Her fans understood her because she spoke, via her characters, like one of them. Lamb Chop, Charlie Horse and Hush Puppy shared in the

FLIP CLIP

remarked. "I think that was part of the magic of Mom's characters."

Lewis perfected her puppet manipulation skills to the point that her soft sidekicks did more than just open and close their mouths to the scripted dialog, they enunciated their words with unprecedented lifelike mouth movement. Coupled with Lewis's deft ventriloquism skill, this facial expressiveness was one of the most significant elements of her act. Puppets and dummies of all types have come and gone over the years, but none has "lived" and "talked" more realistically than those of Shari Lewis. And remember, she did it all with socks.

Television executives were shortsighted about the future value of *The Shari Lewis Show*. Few of the 137 episodes produced between 1960 and 1963 were preserved. Then the show was unceremoniously cancelled; after 1963, instead of Lamb Chop, Charlie Horse and Hush Puppy, viewers found a cartoon show about singing chipmunks in the same time slot. Inexpensive TV animation was becoming all the rage on Saturday mornings. The newest generation of breakfast cereal, fast food and toy consumers—and their dollar-wielding parents—began to choose cartoon shows and superheroes over pliable puppets and educational programming. Such shows prevailed until 1969, when the Public Broadcasting System (PBS) introduced *Sesame Street* and paved the way for Shari Lewis's return to national TV.

Since she had no national TV bookings beyond a smattering of guest appearances

similar experiences of growing up that their audience did, and this led kids to trust and love the plush puppets. In addition, Lewis's delivery of important life lessons avoided the usual authoritative tone; instead she was cast as the best big sister any kid could have. Critics loved the show as much as the kids did: in 1960 *The Shari Lewis Show* won the prestigious Peabody Award from the National Association of Broadcasters, an honor given in recognition of distinguished work in the fields of radio and television broadcasting.

In 1962, during the run of *The Shari Lewis Show*, the busy performer and her husband became the proud parents of a little girl whom they named Mallory. Lamb Chop now had a real-life baby sister, but somehow the puppet remained the baby. "Even when I was very little, I always thought of Lamb Chop as younger than me," Mallory Lewis has since

Though Lewis's national TV program was cancelled in 1965, she never stopped her pattern of hard work and determination, and strived to keep up with the times. The story behind this snapshot from the mid 1960s is unknown, though it's clear the bunny is not a sock puppet.

Flip Clip

On stage in Las Vegas in the mid 1970s, Lewis showed off her considerable singing talents.

NUGGET CIRCUS ROOM THEATER RESTAURANT

As the 1960s came to a close, the glitzy showrooms of Las Vegas offered Shari Lewis and her sock menagerie new outlets to display a wider range of comic material.

during the 1970s and 1980s, it was time to hit the road—and the glitzy showrooms of Lake Tahoe, Reno and Las Vegas. During these years Lewis performed with her puppets in adult venues as the opening act for such luminaries as Jack Benny and Donald O'Connor. Audiences loved the energetic stagecraft she implemented in her act. Lewis danced in a synchronized puppet chorus line, spun about the stage Ginger Rogers-style with a life-sized faux Fred Astaire and, when the spirit moved her, commandeered the conductor's baton and led the band. Best of all, Lewis found that these shows, geared for a more mature crowd, allowed her to make some alterations to the core elements of her act. A more grown-up Shari Lewis now dressed in sexy sequins, choosing elegantly coifed hairstyles and evening gowns over ponytails and poodle skirts. Lamb Chop, Charlie Horse and Hush Puppy— while never using profanity or sexual innuendo

of any kind—could now turn their mischief toward the audience, sometimes leveling jokes and insults worthy of snipester Don Rickles:

> LAMB CHOP: (to a heckler from the audience): *Hey, why are you picking on me? I don't go down to the sewer and bother you while you're working!*

For the next three decades Lewis reinvented herself in a cultural climate that no longer had much interest in ventriloquism. She appeared as a guest star on a range of TV shows, from *I Spy* in the 1960s to *The Nanny* in the 1990s. In an especially exciting 1972 episode (for vent fans, that is) of the series *Love, American Style* entitled "Love and the New Act," Lewis partnered with Paul Winchell in a sketch about two shy ventriloquists who

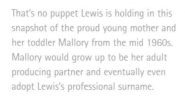

That's no puppet Lewis is holding in this snapshot of the proud young mother and her toddler Mallory from the mid 1960s. Mallory would grow up to be her adult producing partner and eventually even adopt Lewis's professional surname.

a stitch off the old sock

Mallory Lewis, 2001

The night Mallory Lewis and Lamb Chop accepted a posthumous Emmy award for their mother, Shari Lewis, there was not a dry eye in the theater.

Lamb Chop spoke that night, and the mantle was passed. Mallory decided then and there to carry on the life of Shari's little lamb. This decision meant that for the first time a beloved character in the modern vent world would not die with its originator. While others have tried to recreate Bergen's McCarthy and Señor Wences's Pedro and Johnny, no second-generation vent has captured the intent and the style of the original the way Mallory Lewis has. Of course, she comes by it naturally.

Not long after her mother's death, Mallory Lewis realized she could create a very convincing version of Lamb Chop's voice—not Hush Puppy's or Charlie Horse's, just sweet little Lamb Chop's. Then, when she began dabbling in ventriloquism, Lewis found that she had inherited the knack. No lip movement. It was apparent that Lamb Chop could be kept in the family, so there was no reason to deprive the sock puppet's legion of young fans from more entertaining adventures, and no reason to deprive new generations of the wisdom of the curly-haired idol.

Not only did Lewis grow up alongside her mother's puppets, she also worked in her mom's sock-based entertainment empire as early as age twelve. Mallory served as an assistant puppeteer for her mother's early program, *The Shari Show,* and wrote for a Shari Lewis children's column

that was syndicated in newspapers. By the time *Lamb Chop's Play-Along* began its first season in 1992, the younger Lewis was the show's principal writer, eventually graduating to producer by season three. Finally, Lewis was named executive story editor and producer of *The Charlie Horse Music Pizza,* Shari's final series, which was still in production at the time of her mother's death.

Mallory's energy and multiple talents have further proven that she is her mother's daughter in all ways. She is an accomplished author of children's books with bragging rights to twenty published young-adult novels, a number of which have been optioned for television. She is also co-founder—with her husband Brad Hood—of JumpRun Productions, a company which focuses on adventure and extreme sports programming

But Lamb Chop demands most of Mallory's attention. Together they have performed extensively at both live and televised events, at venues that range from Hollywood's Magic Castle to the *QE2*'s stage on a transatlantic crossing. "Mallory is as good with Lamb Chop as her mom was," veteran vent Jimmy Nelson remarked after watching the sister act perform in Las Vegas in 1999. "It was like watching Shari Lewis all over again."

Lewis continues to work with her mother's longtime master puppet maker Pat Brymer and is currently developing a new children's television series starring, of course, the inimitable Lamb Chop. She's creating more

characters, and more venues for them. "I have two new puppets of my own now," Mallory reports. "One is called Zoey, an orangutan character based on my kids book series *Zoey and Me.*" Unlike the sock puppet Lamb Chop, Brymer has fashioned this nearly life-sized playful, furry primate more in the soft, foam and cloth style of the Muppets.

Her other new friend is akin to the family sock puppet legacy. "He's Ram Chop, Lamb Chop's long lost twin brother," Lewis states. Ram Chop is not just a kiddy character— "He's a cocky, tough guy type, with more of a street-wise tone. He's definitely more of a stand-up comedy club puppet."

In 2002 Mallory Lewis and Lamb Chop were prominently featured on a special segment of NBC's *Today Show* about present-day ventriloquists. Appropriately, the piece was hosted by Edgar Bergen's daughter Candice and documented the first meeting of two ventriloquial princesses, the daughters of the king and queen of the art. "We're part of a small, very elite club," Mallory acknowledges. "A lot of ventriloquists have kids, but not all ventriloquists are as legendary as Edgar Bergen and Shari Lewis. How many people can boast Charlie McCarthy or Lamb Chop as their siblings?" As historic events go, the Bergen-Lewis introduction was perhaps only one short segment for a network morning show, but it was a gigantic moment for every fan of ventriloquism.

Lewis appeared at the
White House in 1978 as
part of a presidential
command performance.
Here, President Jimmy
Carter shows his
appreciation.

communicate through their dummies. In yet
another impressive display of versatility, she
and her husband Jeremy co-wrote an episode
of the original 1970s *Star Trek* series entitled
"The Lights of Zetar."

All the while, Lewis and her puppets
managed to continue securing bookings in venues throughout the U.S. and Europe. They even
co-hosted the occasional network TV special or
holiday parade broadcast. Though the popular
tide had turned away from the art of ventriloquism, Lewis—always the go-getter—kept as
active as possible. While most of her vent peers
were being relegated to county fair and trade
show gigs, Lewis remained characteristically
undaunted, never fully fading from the legiti-
mate spotlight. That Lewis fans remained loyal
to her is demonstrated by the numerous honors
she received during this period, including a 1974
Emmy for an NBC special called *A Picture of Us*
and the prestigious Kennedy Center Award for
Creativity in the Arts in 1983.

Throughout the 1980s, Lewis continued
this serious game of show business survival,
traveling almost constantly, always in search
of new avenues to ply her talents and stay in
the public eye, be it through her writing, acting or dancing. She never compromised her
integrity as a top-notch professional, and audiences rewarded her performances with thun-
derous ovations. But in 1984 the term "survival"
had a different meaning when she was diagnosed with breast cancer. The boundless
courage Shari Lewis had always exhibited pro-

fessionally was put to the test by this personal
tragedy. In a nearly miraculous testament to
her positive fortitude and will, she successfully
fought the disease and won without surgery,
choosing a health regime incorporating vita-
mins, diet and exercise.

In 1992, after nearly two decades of
taking her multi-faceted talents on and off the
road, Lewis's TV career once again began to
flourish. PBS began airing a show Lewis had
originally developed as a very successful video
in the late 1980s. The energetic and educational *Lamb Chop's Play-Along!* proved perfect for
public television's long established *Sesame
Street* demographic. But the kids in the studio
audience of this later era demanded more
entertainment than just a lady with a cute
puppet on her hand. And of course, Lewis had
big ambitions and goals for her new show—
she wanted more flexibility of movement for
her characters.

Because it was produced on the shoe-
string budget typical of most public television
programs, the show proved to be a production
challenge. "We did a whole lot with a whole little," recalls Pat Brymer, Lewis's longtime master
puppet maker, who ingeniously created new
versions of Lamb Chop, Charlie Horse and Hush
Puppy that could ride bikes, dance and do flips.
Lamb Chop's Play-Along! featured songs and
activities designed to stimulate young viewers to
interact with the characters. Lewis described it
concisely: "I call it an 'anti-couch potato' show."
It all proved delightful enough to TV audiences

to garner five consecutive Emmy awards in the "Outstanding Performer in a Children's Series" category from 1992 through 1996.

Lamb Chop's Play-Along! ended its broadcast run in early 1998 and was almost immediately replaced by *The Charlie Horse Music Pizza*. "We felt, simply, that Lamb Chop was well established enough that we could bring Charlie Horse into the forefront for a change," Mallory Lewis explains. "It was his turn, so to speak." The show was a children's musical sit-com, of sorts, set in an imaginary pizzeria and starring Lewis with her usual cast of characters. The new show was well on its way to becoming as successful as any of Shari Lewis's previous ventures when tragedy occurred: she was diagnosed with terminal uterine cancer.

Lewis insisted that "the show must go on" and chose not to tell her show's crew about her illness. While secretly undergoing radiation treatments and chemotherapy, she continued to work through the summer, completing a full season of shows.

For the final episode of the season, she sang "Hello—Goodbye," a song about the difference in the two words' meanings, with Lamb Chop, Charlie Horse and Hush Puppy. After the taping, she called the cast and crew together, gently explained why she would not be return-ing next year and quietly departed the sound stage. Two weeks later, on August 2, 1998, Shari Lewis passed away. She was sixty-five years old.

Lewis's twelfth Emmy in the "Outstand-ing Performer in a Children's Series" category was awarded posthumously in 2000. Mallory Lewis accepted the award on her mother's behalf and brought along Lamb Chop as a treat for the audience. When the proud daughter reached the podium, she thanked the television academy for honoring her mother, then, impul-sively, asked the sock puppet on her hand if she had anything to say. Fighting back tears, Mallory Lewis helped the tiny lamb mutter in a familiar voice, "Shari would be so happy."

Upon hearing of the 1972 death of longtime friend and pen pal, Vent Haven's W.S. Berger, Shari Lewis sent this inscribed photo of herself and Lamb Chop to be added to the Kentucky museum's permanent collection. According to letters dated as early as 1953, Lewis and Berger had for years maintained a close correspondence.

Flip Clip

DUMMY DATA

NAME: **SAMSON**

ARRIVED ON THE SCENE:
around 1945

DISTINGUISHING
CHARACTERISTICS:
curly hair, sycophantic
tendencies

Given to Lewis by her
magician father, Samson
was her very first ventriloquist dummy. The dummy
was a fast-talking, deal-
making show biz agent,
who could realistically
smoke a cigar.

FAMED REMARK: "Stick
with me, kid, an' da' sky's
da' limit!"

NAME: **BUTTERCUP**

ARRIVED ON THE SCENE:
late 1940s

DISTINGUISHING
CHARACTERISTICS:
blond hair

Little is remembered about
this girl dummy, who
posed with Lewis in several publicity photos in the
late 1940s and early
1950s. Buttercup made
some early local New York
TV appearances with the
young vent.

NAME: **TAFFY TWINKLE**

ARRIVED ON THE SCENE:
early 1950s

DISTINGUISHING
CHARACTERISTICS:
Lewis's Taffy was a silly
farm girl who appeared,
often along with her
brother, Dinky, on many of
the vent's early TV shows.
On *Facts 'n' Fun with Shari
Lewis* Taffy and Lewis
would sing songs, play
games and tell stories.
The dummy was also
featured on *Arthur
Godfrey's Talent Scouts* in
1952 and on *Shari and
Her Friends* from 1953
to 1955.

NAME: **DINKY TWINKLE**

ARRIVED ON THE SCENE:
early 1950s

DISTINGUISHING
CHARACTERISTICS:
looked an awful lot like
Samson

Based on publicity shots
from the period, it appears
that this figure, called
Dinky, was a recycled
Samson—Lewis's first
dummy from the mid
1940s. If not, then Samson
and Dinky were certainly
identical twins.

NAME: **LAMB CHOP**

ARRIVED ON THE SCENE:
1955

DISTINGUISHING
CHARACTERISTICS:
mushy mouth, sleepy eyes
with mink lashes, floppy
ears, red mittens (a lamb
who knew how to
accessorize)

The shy, soft-spoken, six-
year-old Lamb Chop was
introduced to TV viewers
on *Captain Kangaroo* and
taught four generations
of TV viewers important
lessons and endless knock-
knock jokes. Aside from
being a TV star, Lamb Chop
also addressed a House
subcommittee on Capitol
Hill in 1993, encouraging
it to pass a bill to improve
children's television
programming.

FAMED REMARK: "Alphabet
soup is very educational."

FLIP CLIP

NAME: **CHARLIE HORSE**

ARRIVED ON THE SCENE:
1955

DISTINGUISHING
CHARACTERISTICS:
buck teeth, straw hat and
pointed ears

This streetwise sock puppet
pony came into existence
soon after Lamb Chop and
served as the little lamb's
ten-year-old big brother.
Charlie Horse remained a
regular in Lewis's act until
the ventriloquist's death in
1998 and even had his
own show, *The Charlie
Horse Music Pizza.*

NAME: **HUSH PUPPY**

ARRIVED ON THE SCENE:
1955

DISTINGUISHING
CHARACTERISTICS:
floppy ears, little black
nose perched precariously
far on his little face,
occasional bow tie,
southern accent

This southern-fried sock
puppet pooch was Lewis's
version of the country
cousin character. Hush
Puppy was created at the
same time as her "older
brother" Charlie Horse and
"little sister" Lamb Chop
and became a standard
and much-beloved member
of Lewis's plush cast.

NAME: **MEOW MEOW**

ARRIVED ON THE SCENE:
mid 1960s

DISTINGUISHING
CHARACTERISTICS:
fuzzy fur coat, big eyes,
a name that is really
fun to say

Sadly, this wild-looking
plush cat puppet never
really caught on with
audiences and was rarely
seen in Lewis's act.

NAME: **SEYMOUR**

ARRIVED ON THE SCENE:
unknown

DISTINGUISHING
CHARACTERISTICS:
he's a ping-pong ball

Seymour is indicative of
the many lesser-known
characters Shari Lewis
used. Others were more
elaborate, including
a wonderful life-sized
dancing Fred Astaire and a
Rockette-style chorus line
of high-kicking female
dummies. Lewis's other
minor puppet characters
included Wing Ding,
Grizzley, Mr. Bearly,
Honey Childs, Bella and
Nevil the Devil.

FAMED REMARKS:

CHARLIE HORSE: *That's the silliest joke I've ever heard!*

HUSH PUPPY: *And you're the silliest horse I've ever seen,
so we're even!*

where have all the dummies gone?

The Story of W.S. Berger and the Vent Haven Museum

Picture the town of Fort Mitchell, a tiny dot on the map of northern Kentucky two miles from Cincinnati. Midwestern working-class neighborhood streets are lined with quaint two-story red brick homes. A paper boy rides by on his shiny new Schwinn, his aim accurate as he tosses the morning news onto each front porch. Kids walk to school as their proud parents prepare for the day—a scene right out of Norman Rockwell. Fort Mitchell is one of those sleepy hamlets where clocks seem to tick a little slower.

Since 1972, the Vent Haven Museum has stood at 33 West Maple Avenue, housing the largest collection of ventriloquial material in the world. Some five hundred retired professional dummies reside there, including specially made museum replicas of Charlie McCarthy, Mortimer Snerd, Effie Klinker, Jerry Mahoney and Knucklehead Smiff. A tattered decoy version of Jimmy Nelson's Farfel is there, which the great vent once used as a stunt double in his famous Nestle's TV commercials.

An entire corner is devoted to Frank Marshall, creator of Danny O'Day, Jerry Mahoney and thousands of less famous figures. His woodworking tools and many unfinished dummy heads sit forever displayed behind glass.

On the shelves stand hundreds of volumes on ventriloquism, including books in eight languages that date back to the eighteenth century. The library also contains ventriloquism mail-order courses, sheet music and scripts dating back to turn-of-the-century vaudeville skits. There are also publicity pamphlets, vintage playbills and records, as well as tape

Along with the complete dummies, Berger's collection also featured many disembodied wooden heads displayed on specially made shelves. Some of these hand-carved works of art date to the mid nineteenth century and the earliest days of vaudeville.

W.S. Berger poses with only part of his massive collection of figures and vent memorabilia. This photo was probably taken in the late 1940s, soon after Berger renovated his one-car garage into a new home for orphaned dummies. Though Berger always welcomed unannounced guests to view his collection, few of his immediate neighbors were even aware of its existence until after his 1972 death, when his home was designated as a museum.

recordings of performances and interviews with ventriloquists from all over the world.

But the most intriguing feature of all is the fact that Vent Haven Museum evolved from one man's sixty-year obsession with dummies. William Shakespeare Berger hadn't even seen a ventriloquist act until he was in his thirties— but once he did, he was hooked.

Berger's fascination cannot be classified as a mere hobby, nor dismissed as an eccentricity. The man was on a mission: to make certain that orphaned ventriloquist dummies would never be forgotten or forsaken. Berger's passion for dummies was ignited in 1910 while he was in New York City. After seeing his first ventriloquist, Harry "The Great" Lester, Berger was mesmerized and insisted on meeting the

performer. The two men struck up a fast and loyal friendship, the first of Berger's many relationships with belly speakers, famous or otherwise, from around the world.

On that same trip Berger bought his first dummy, which he named Tommy Baloney. Though he never became a professional ventriloquist, his love for the craft drove him to purchase more puppets and learn as much about them as he could. Friends observed that he seemed to see a human face behind every dummy, and they weren't too surprised when he became obsessed with the fates of dummies that outlived their owners.

Berger enthusiastically began collecting figures and memorabilia relating to ventriloquial arts. His unique collection gained such a

Flip Clip

respected reputation in ventriloquist circles, that soon many retiring vaudevillian vents bequeathed their figures to him. Eventually the dummies took up too much room—they were arranged on every available surface, from the living room to the kitchen. To solve the problem, Berger renovated his garage to house his prized possessions and constructed two additional buildings on his property, creating a place he called Vent Haven. As he envisioned it, the compound would serve as a retirement home for any ventriloquist's dummy in need of a final resting place.

From the late 1940s until 1960, Berger was the president of the International Brotherhood of Ventriloquists. His leadership helped the fringe organization grow to a membership one thousand strong. He also published a monthly newsletter, *The Oracle*, and maintained extensive personal correspondence with ventriloquists around the world. His letters became part of an archive that contains responses from such vent luminaries as Edgar Bergen, Paul Winchell, Señor Wences, Jimmy Nelson and Shari Lewis, among many others. Since Berger's death in 1972, the museum has

At one point, virtually every corner of Berger's home was taken up by dummies. This undated photo, probably from the early 1940s, was taken in the collector's living room. Frank Marshall made the carved wooden Punch-and-Judy hand puppets he holds. The puppets remain on display today at Vent Haven Museum.

One of the many thousands of vintage vent-related photographs from Berger's collection. This undated shot features a young Ed Sullivan (at left, holding hammer and champagne bottle) clowning around with vaudeville vent "The Great Lester" (second from left with dummy).

continued to exist as a nonprofit organization.

In 1975 Vent Haven Museum began hosting the annual International Ventriloquist's Convention. That first convention featured special performances by Edgar Bergen and Jimmy Nelson. Now under the direction of professional vent Mark Wade, the IVC is the largest and oldest continuously running vent gathering.

To visit Vent Haven is an almost mystical experience. The hundreds of dummies housed there, forever resting on their little chairs and inside their glass cabinets, evoke a quiet sense of past achievement one must experience personally to fully appreciate. Vent Haven is a monument to a unique folk art and without doubt an oddly wonderful place to experience

the world of ventriloquism. And more than a quarter of a century after Berger's death, no dummy without a home is ever turned away.

Berger amassed over five hundred ventriloquist figures between 1910 and his death at age ninety-two in 1972.

afterword

Ventriloquism . . . from my corner of the stage

I've been a ventriloquist since the age of eight. My wife likes what I do for a living, and ventriloquism is what allowed us to meet in the first place. But not long ago she finally asked the question no one else ever had: "Didn't you get made fun of in school because of the dummies? Weren't you a geek?" Gulp. What!? I had always thought it was the exact opposite: I stood out from the crowd some-how *because* I was a ventriloquist, and that being unique was a good thing. They sure as heck applauded big-time at the talent shows. But as I look back, I wonder how many kids snickered behind my back. I've never heard of a ventriloquist getting beat up on the playground.

This quirky little art form has been a part of my life every day since Christmas 1969,

when I got my first vent figure. It was a vinyl Juro Celebrity Mortimer Snerd. To help me learn the skill, my parents bought me Jimmy Nelson's record, *Instant Ventriloquism*. Hour after hour I would sit down with Jimmy and Danny O'Day and Farfel, listening to the record, practicing and practicing, until I thought I was good enough to do a real show. (And by the way, there's never been a better, simpler, more fun way to learn ventriloquism than Jimmy's album. I wore that thing out.)

Edgar Bergen and Jimmy Nelson were my two earliest mentors. I studied daily with Jimmy on his record, then was excited beyond belief to meet him for the first time at the 1975 Vent Haven International Ventriloquist's Convention. Bergen I met only once, but I would listen to his taped radio broadcasts over and over, emulating the comedy. I would even start and stop the cassettes, writing out the dialog word for word, discovering what Charlie and Mortimer's words looked like in script form. This is where I learned to appreciate the con-struction of jokes and sharp dialog. Bergen brought ventriloquism out of the mire of vaude-ville and proved to the world that talking dum-mies could be a first-class form of entertainment.

After Bergen, Paul Winchell and Jimmy Nelson made ventriloquism appealing to a whole new generation by taking advantage of this new thing called television. I was a bit on

Eight-year-old Jeff Dunham with his Juro Mortimer Snerd doll in 1969.

124

the young side to have seen either Jimmy or Paul live on TV, but it's obvious from the few tapes of Winchell's Saturday morning TV show, as well as Nelson's Nestle's and Texaco commercials, that kid after kid became enamored with making a dummy talk. With toy dummies of each of their characters readily available, many aspiring young vents gained self-confidence by learning ventriloquism and performing at schools, churches, scouting functions and birthday parties. As for Shari Lewis, Lamb Chop was second only to Kermit the Frog when it came to being the most famous and beloved talking piece of cloth. But what many people didn't see was Shari's innovation in taking ventriloquism to a higher level. She shined brightest in concert, proving that ventriloquism could be the hub of a big show.

I caught Señor Wences a couple of times on Ed Sullivan's show and saw him live once. He had an absolutely flawless act. It was perfect in the same way that a ballet is perfect. The timing had been honed and perfected over decades of doing the exact same material over and over. There was no fat—no superfluous movement, no unnecessary words in his performance. This act was so perfect that Señor Wences could do exactly the same routines in multiple languages . . . and get the same big laughs. I have enough trouble getting people to chuckle in English.

Jeff Dunham and Walter in 2003.

Now, more than three decades since I began, I look at my own characters, Peanut, Walter, and José Jalapeño on a Stick, and I realize how much fun all this still is. Every day I think about ventriloquism, and every day I work at it. Ventriloquism has been a source of enjoyment and a vehicle of opportunity for me. But there is a weird part that goes along with all this . . . Sometimes I wonder if I really own my house and all my possessions . . . I figure that really, Peanut, Walter and José do. They're the ones who get all the laughs. I'm still the geek with a talking doll.

—JEFF DUNHAM

Flip Clip

bibliography

books

Bergen, Candice. *Knock Wood.*
New York City, NY: Linden Press/
Simon and Schuster, 1984.

Bergen, Edgar. *How to Become a
Ventriloquist.* New York City, NY:
Grosset & Dunlap, 1938/Mineola,
NY: Dover Publications, 2000.

Brose, Mike. *Figure Making Can
Be Fun?!? A Complete Guide to
Making a 'Professional Ventriloquist
Figure'.* Barnum, MN: Puppets and
Props Publishing, 2001.

Burns, Stanley. *Other Voices:
Ventriloquism from BC to TV.*
USA: Sylvia Burns, 2000.

Shulman, Arthur and Youman,
Roger. *How Sweet It Was; Television:
A Pictorial Commentary.* New York
City, NY: Shorecrest, 1966.

Vox, Valentine. *I Can See Your Lips
Moving: The History and Art of
Ventriloquism.* Tadworth, Surrey
(UK): Kaye & Ward, 1981/Studio
City, CA: Players Press, 1993.

Wade, Mark. *Kid Show
Ventriloquism.* Tavares, FL:
SPS Publications, 1996.

Winchell, Paul. *Ventriloquism for
Fun and Profit.* Baltimore, MD:
I.&M. Ottenheimer, 1954.

magazines/periodicals

The Barker Magazine
Norcross, GA, 2000-2002
Bob Abdou, Publisher

Dialogue
The Ventriloquist World
Association
New Jersey, 1981-1999
Bob Ladd, Publisher.

The Puppet Collector's Newsletter
Issue #3, March 1997
Venice, CA.
Steve Meltzer, Publisher.

The Oracle
International Brotherhood
of Ventriloquists
Fort Mitchell, KY, 1950-1960
W.S. Berger, Publisher

The New Oracle
Society of American Ventriloquists
Baltimore, MD, 1976-1986
Mark Wade, Publisher.

The Saturday Evening Post
"Secrets of the Talking Dummies"
Rufus Jarman; May 9, 1953

Vent-O-Gram
San Francisco, CA, 1963-1969.

The New Vent-O-Gram
International Ventriloquists
Association
Illinois, 1970-1984.

videotapes/films

The American Puppet
Bristol, CT: Mazzarella Bros.
Productions, Inc., 2001.

The Best of Paul Winchell
Paul Winchell, 1998.

*Biography: Edgar Bergen,
His Many Voices*
A&E Network/Peter Jones
Productions, 1995

*Biography: Shari Lewis and
Lamb Chop*
A&E Network/Weller/Grossman
Productions, 1994

Pat Brymer: Master Puppeteer
Courtesy of Pat Brymer

Fun and Fancy Free
Walt Disney Pictures, 1947
Courtesy of Doug Preis

*The Jimmy Nelson Nestle's
Commericals: 1955-1965*
Courtesy of Jimmy Nelson

The Operation
Vitaphone short film,
Warner Bros., 1930
Courtesy of Doug Preis

Highlights from
The Ed Sullivan Show
Courtesy of Jimmy Nelson

A Tribute to Shari Lewis
PBS, 1998

You Can't Cheat an Honest Man
Universal Pictures, 1939
Courtesy of Doug Preis

museum

The Vent Haven Museum
(open May 1 through
September 30)
33 West Maple Avenue
Fort Mitchell, KY 41011
phone: 859-341-0461
e-mail: venthaven@insightbb.com

web sites

The Internet Movie Database:
www.imdb.com

Puppetolio!
www.puppetmagic.com

Snerdville:
www.fathom.org/snerdville

TV Tome:
www.tvtome.com

Vent Haven:
www.venthaven.com

Paul Winchell:
www.paulwinchell.com

acknowledgments

FLIP CLIP

Few books are executed by only one individual—especially those like this one, which required scores of interviews, volumes of research and endless navigation through oceans of visual material. I could never have undertaken this five-year journey of discovery without the help and unwavering enthusiasm of the following people, to whom I am eternally grateful and none of whom is a dummy:

Paddy Calistro: The angelic driving force behind Angel City Press who from the beginning, for reasons unknown, trusted that I wasn't a flake and, for the love of Farfel, took on the task of publishing this book. Paddy, you're more than a master publisher; you're a partner and a friend.

And Paddy's Angels: Andrea Richards, my stalwart editor who helped me find and maintain my writer's voice. You're the keeper of clarity in my text. Scott McAuley, your constant smile is worth the over thirty thousand words you read. You possess the brain I'll never have. Amy Inouye, your artistry with graphics and typography actually create the illusion that I'm hip. A major feat in and of itself. Ailene Kanbe, your astute eye helped my words stay lively and on target. Sheila Perkins, your positive energy made every phone call a comforting pleasure.

Leonard Maltin, whose admiration and respect for the art of ventriloquism, conveyed so eloquently in his generous Foreword, added invaluably to this book.

Betty and Jimmy Nelson, whose patience, trust and openness were my engine, supporting me through this entire, long ride. This book would not have come to pass without your commitment and generosity. And a big thank-you to the whole Nelson brood: Larry, Jerry, Leejay, Marianne, Elizabeth and Jim Jr. You define the word "family" and you never made me feel like an intruder.

Frances Bergen, whose stories from her incredible life conveyed the dignified, utterly class act that Edgar Bergen was. Kris Bergen, whose fond memories of his beloved father

added the necessary humanity to my research.

Megan and Doug Preis, thank you for sacrificing an entire Labor Day weekend to allow me to pillage your amazing Bergen treasure trove of photos, puppets and memorabilia. It's been a fun five years of phone calls and e-mails. Let's keep it going.

Dr. Paul Winchell, who granted me hours of enthralling interviews, e-mails and photographs, filling in all the blanks in the kind of extraordinary life story most folks only dream of living. Burt DuBrow, whose devotion to everything-Winchell brought insight and accuracy to my story of Winch. Paul "Alf" Fusco, you are living proof that a puppet-loving kid can grow up to be a professional puppet-loving adult.

Natalie "Taly" Moreno, whose memories of her husband Señor Wences confirm him as the true artist that he was. Lupé and Norm Nielsen, thank you for opening your home to me, affording me a unique glimpse into Wences's magic world.

Mallory Lewis: Energy and vitality such as yours can only run in the family. The pleasure of knowing you is to get a fair idea of your mother's bright, tireless star. Pat Brymer, master puppeteer and maker of living souls from cloth and foam: Your love for Shari is evident in every stitch. Richard Seymour and Kevin Butler, thank you for providing the type of brass-tacks information I needed to tell Shari's story.

All my friends associated with the amazing Vent Haven Museum and the annual Vent Haven International Ventriloquist's Convention, especially curator Lisa Sweasy and her husband Bryan Sweasy, Museum Board of Directors members John R.S. Brooking, Charlotte Brooking, Don W. Millure, Dorothy Millure, John S. Brooking, Annie B. Roberts and convention director Mark Wade. You opened your doors to me, providing a research source unequaled anywhere. I feel certain W.S. Berger is smiling down on you all.

My new pals in the ventriloquial

community, who took the time to sit and chat, lending invaluable knowledge, photos, stories, advice, philosophies, opinions and enthusiasm to my research. You are the lifeblood of this book: Bob Abdou, Fred Anderson, Tom Basso, Mike Brose, Marlene Clark, Harold Crocker, Bill DeMar, Clinton Detweiler, Paige and Jeff Dunham, Michael Eakins, Dick Fitzmaurice, Al Getler, Carol Greene, Barbara and Ray Guyll, Conrad Hartz, Linda Holliday, Bob Issacson, Bob Ladd, Tom Ladshaw, Les Lamborn, Jerry Layne, Cy Leonard, Mark Lewis, Johnnie Main, Steve Meltzer, Pete Michaels, Carla Rhodes, Dan Ritchard, Bob Rhumba, Alan Semok, Al Stevens, Mike Valentine and Bruce Weaver. If there is anyone I've forgotten, I love you, too, and beg forgiveness.

And to the kind folks who helped in so many different ways, be it by contributing ideas, quotes, research material, transcribing interview tapes, mailing packages, organizing files or just acting like they thought this book was a good idea. I love you all: Wendy Backe, Ken Bruce, Cody Cameron, Kevin Lima and Brenda Chapman, Jason Clark, Nell Clark, Lorna Cook, Matt Davis, Ron Davis, Warren Davis, Kevin Engle, Nick Fletcher, Bobreta Franklin, John Fusco, Frank Gladstone, Ryan Harris, Jeffrey Katzenberg, Fumi Kitahara, Lane Smith and Molly Leach, Gianpierro "Bud" Leone, John Levin, Minnie McMillan, Rob Minkoff, Nancy Newhouse-Porter, Pattee and Jerry Newman, Alina Phelan, Jill Ragaway, Carin Sage, Michael Saltzman, Joseph R. Thygesen, Bob Tzutiker and Noni White, Conrad Vernon, and, of course, my Big Sis Gwen and her hubby Howard Speed.

And, speaking of love, a special thanks to my spouse and best friend, Loretta Weeks, who remained by my side for the duration of this five-year project, despite the times it must have seemed that I was surely descending into madness.

—KELLY ASBURY

photo credits

The publisher thanks the following people and institutions for providing the rights to reproduce the images in this book.

Kelly Asbury: 5 (right), 15 (photo by Gianpierro "Bud" Leone), 65, 128

Burt DuBrow: 6 (top right), 12, 59, 60 (left), 62 (left), 67 (right), 68, 69 (top left and right), 70, 72, 73 (right), 75, two Winchell flip clips

Jeff Dunham: 124

Michael Eakins: 99 (bottom right)

Dick Fitzmaurice: 96 (bottom right)

Al Getler: 4 (top left)

Conrad Hartz: 96 (bottom center)

Linda Holliday: 4 (middle right)

Tom Ladshaw: 2 (top right), 2 (third row), 11, 41 (left), 42, 43, 53, 57, 58, 60 (top right), 61, 62 (top right), 63, 67 (left), 74, 96 (bottom left), 98

Mallory Lewis: 2 (second row right), 7, 103-107 (bottom), 108-116, 118 (far right), 119, Lewis flip clip

Leonard Maltin: 8-9

Pete Michaels: 99 (bottom left)

Betty and Jimmy Nelson: 2 (bottom), 5 (left), 6 (bottom right), 13, 77-91, 93-95, 96 (top left), 97-98, 99 (top right), 101 (right), Farfel flip clip

Norm Nielsen: 6 (center), 39, 41 (right), 44-47, 49-51

Doug Preis: 2 (second row left), 6 (top left), 10, 17-35, 37, two Bergen flip clips

Vent Haven Museum: 14, 40, 54, 64, 92, 100 (left), 101, 107 (top left and right), 117, 118 (all but Lamb Chop), 120-123

Michael Valentine: 4 (bottom left)

Bruce Weaver: 99 (bottom center)

Paul Winchell: 48, 73 (top)

Book jacket:
Burt DuBrow:
front cover (images 4 and 8)
Tom Ladshaw:
front cover (image 2), back cover (image 5)
Mallory Lewis:
front cover (images 6 and 11), back cover (image 2)

Betty and Jimmy Nelson:
front cover (images 5 and 10), back cover (image 1)
Norm Nielsen:
front cover (image 9), back cover (image 3)
Doug Preis:
front cover (images 1, 3 and 7), back cover (image 4)

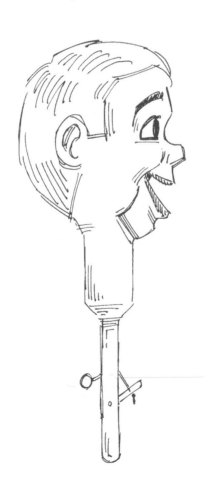

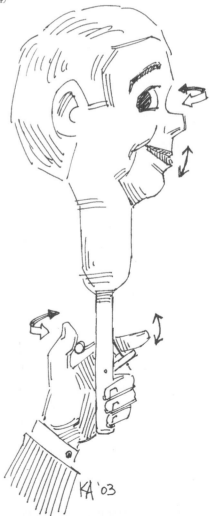

KA '03

Close de door!